Sold Out

The True Cost of Supermarket Shopping

William Young

For Sarah and my family

First published in 2004 by Vision Paperbacks,
a division of Satin Publications Ltd.
101 Southwark Street
London SE1 0JF
UK
info@visionpaperbacks.co.uk
www.visionpaperbacks.co.uk
Publisher: Sheena Dewan

A catalogue record for this book is available from the British Library.

ISBN: 1-904132-40-5

2 4 6 8 10 9 7 5 3 1

Cover photo: Ghislain & Marie David de Lossy/Getty Images
Cover and text design by ok?design
Printed and bound in the UK by
Mackays of Chatham Ltd, Chatham, Kent.

Contents

List of Figures and Tables

Preface

When people go food shopping, they almost always go to a supermarket. Over 95 per cent of people do their main shopping at a supermarket, and there are no signs that this is going to change in the near future.[1] Demos, the London-based think tank describes the rise of this supermarket culture:

> *Many aspects of food have improved since the end of the Second World War. The level and range of affordable nutrition, and the global cuisine that we now access through television, supermarkets and high-street restaurants, reflect significant progress. Advances in agricultural technology and management have brought more plentiful, cheaper and more hygienic food to the mass of the population. As British society has grown more affluent, food culture has taken on an increasingly 'postmaterialist' complexion, serving needs well beyond simple survival. It is still less than 50 years since rationing ended in the UK but, within that time, supermarkets have become secular cathedrals, offering to meet all our lifestyle needs, expanding into banking, dating, childcare and learning provision, and developing around them a*

> *host of hangers-on, cultish visionaries and*
> *oppositional forces. As a result, they have*
> *acquired an almost mythical significance in*
> *the public image.*[2]

This gives supermarkets significant influence over consumers, farmers, communities, workers in developing countries, the environment and the food we eat. The dominance of large supermarket chains affects every area of our lives; economically, socially, environmentally and culturally. While supermarkets have undoubtedly brought many benefits, their dominance creates problems.[3] Someone pays for the consequences of 'low, low' prices in supermarkets, which woo and captivate consumers. Even government policies only aim to encourage cheap supermarket food at the expense of society and the environment, and are absurdly biased towards the supermarkets.[4]

This book investigates the devastating impacts of supermarkets on suppliers and farmers, communities, the environment, what we actually eat, and their employees and workers. The first chapter charts the extraordinary supermarket revolution. It explains which supermarkets dominate in the UK, Europe and globally, and explores the origins of each of the main supermarkets. The second chapter explores some of the most common allegations against supermarkets; their consistent bullying of suppliers and farmers and abuse of their huge buying power, and the failure of the government to implement a meaningful code of practice. Chapter 3 looks at the impacts of supermarkets on communities, and Chapter 4 examines their potential to harm our environment.

Chapter 5 looks at supermarket food, and how fatty and sugary processed foods are affecting our children's health. The following chapter concentrates on the conditions – if not exploitation – of supermarket employees and workers, versus 'fat cat' salaries for those at the top. In Chapter 7, I examine the power and profits of supermarkets. The world's largest company in 2003 was a supermarket, with US $244 billion[5] worth of sales. The final chapter considers whether supermarkets are simply the product of the society we live in or, more sinisterly, have enormous companies developed a life and momentum of their own, beyond our control?

Consumers need to wake up to the fact that problems they see in their local communities are linked to their obsession with supermarkets. As such, we all pay the high price of supermarket shopping. It is time to ensure that the changes of the next 30 years are in the public interest and are environmentally and socially responsible on a global basis.[6] Consumers need to start to change their shopping habits to include a varied diet of local independent retailers and markets as well as supermarkets. Finally, supermarkets, governments and consumers need to take responsibility and reverse the negative effects of our food-shopping monoculture. We are addicted to the seductive allure of supermarkets; their convenience, bright lights, colourful packaging and promise of unbeatable, cheap prices. We need to see the reality; ruthless multinational companies who are set on profits and market domination.

The writing of this book involved many people to whom I am most grateful. Firstly, the School of the Environment, University of Leeds, for allowing me the time and space to write the book; to Sarah Young, Jean Young, Louise Ellis and my parents for proofreading the manuscript; to Jean Young for producing the index; to Liz Puttick and my publishers for the opportunity to write this book; and to my family, friends and colleagues for their encouragement.

As with a book of this nature, there are the disclaimers. Firstly, the views expressed in this book are solely the author's and are not the views held by the University of Leeds, Elizabeth Puttick Literary Agency or the publishers. Any errors and omissions are the responsibility of the author and the information in this book is as current as reasonably possible at publication.

William Young

Chapter 1

Who Are the Supermarkets?

The face of grocery shopping has changed dramatically over the last 50 years: from a multitude of local shops serving over the counter, to a handful of self-service supermarkets. These stores dominate not just the grocery market but also, increasingly, other areas, from clothes to financial services. In 2003, the largest company in the world was the supermarket group Wal-Mart, with US $244 billion worth of sales. Supermarkets have become multinational companies by taking control of whole supply chains and operating in increasing numbers of countries. This chapter charts the extraordinary revolution in grocery shopping over the past 150 years.

Shopping in the 1850s

Back in the 1850s, a walk to the shops for the wealthy, according to Seth and Randall in their book The *Grocers*, meant visiting grocers selling traditional food-stuffs, from sugar to spices, tea, cocoa and coffee, and buying from farmers selling fresh eggs, butter, cheese and bacon in open-air markets or specialist cheese-mongers. The ubiquitous oil and colourman sold an incredible range of products, including paints, oils, soap, candles, starch, matches, firewood, brushes, baskets, brooms, petroleum, lamps, linseed oil beeswax and vegetable wax, gums and resins. You could also buy sauces, pickles and jams, chemicals and drugs such as soda, Glauber's salts, quack pills and poor man's plaster, and commodities including hardware, ironmongery, china, lampblack, size, ochre, chalk, sand, vitriol, brick dust, and gunpowder and shot. Italian warehousemen specialised in imported olive oil, nut oil and items such as macaroni and vermicelli.[2]

Grocers, like other retailers, were skilled craftsmen who ran their businesses as such. They would own the business, which would pass from father to son (who served an apprenticeship), and they would live on the premises. They chopped or pounded by hand the cones of sugar, ground and mixed spices, and chose and blended teas. Success depended on reputation and was based on quality of goods and honesty. Today, we would find the shops unattractive and dimly lit, unlike our supermarkets, with no concept of display.[3]

The working class in the 1850s would only purchase bare necessities from the grocer, preferring to buy from open markets, or from the market halls that were springing up in cities. Until it was made illegal, industrial workers would buy much of what they needed from 'truck' shops owned by their employer. Opportunities for cheating – adulterating or stinting on measures – were always present because grocers prepared so much of the final product. Also prices were rarely fixed and displayed, so haggling ('higgling' or 'chaffering') was very much the order of the day.[4]

The Industrial Revolution, however, had an important impact on the development of retailing and grocers:[5]

- The new industrialised working class now demanded mass consumer goods.

- The new urban middle class demanded a better shopping experience.

- A new supply chain for products was needed because of the decline of British agriculture and the availability of cheap food from abroad.

- Mass production of consumer goods started to take off.

- Real income per head almost doubled and consumers started demanding cheap new products.

Many grocers started to become self-service as a result of the increase in school-leaver age, which reduced the supply of cheap labour, and there was also a slow rise in the size of some shops through mergers and organic growth.[6] By the end of the Second World War, the grocery industry had moved towards cleaner, brighter shops advertising products and services.

The expansion of the supermarket

In the 1970s, grocers discovered the full benefits from increasing in size, and began the trend that continued for decades: the total number of shops declined but the average size increased. In one year alone, 1978–79, the new 'supermarkets' closed over 350 shops smaller than 5,000 square feet and opened 60 of more than 10,000. Over the period 1971–79, the total number of grocery shops fell from 105,283 to 68,567, a decline of 35 per cent; for the multiples the decrease was 45 per cent. Those who recognised its potential applied the logic of size remorselessly, and superstores (25,000 square feet or more) and hypermarkets (50,000 square feet or more)[7] began to appear.

The graph below illustrates the dramatic transformation of the British grocery market between 1965 and 1998. It shows that:

- **The biggest player in 1965, the co-operative movement, shrank from over 35 per cent to less than 10 per cent of the market.**

- **The 'independents and others' sector, which started the period with more than 50 per cent, ended at under 15 per cent.**

The big winners were Tesco and Sainsbury's, followed by Asda and Safeway; altogether these supermarkets have now some two-thirds of the market.[8]

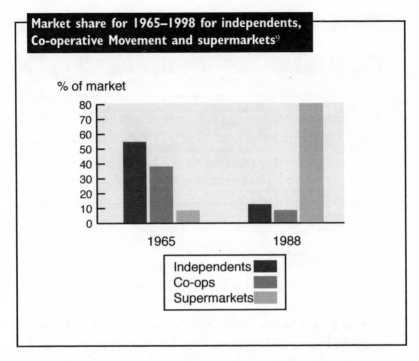

Market share for 1965–1998 for independents, Co-operative Movement and supermarkets[9]

% of market

Independents
Co-ops
Supermarkets

Today, the supermarkets are in 'takeover fever', battling not only with other supermarkets, such as Safeway, but with independent chains that they then convert to their own brand. This process started in the 1990s with supermarkets' own 'express' formats – smaller versions of the supermarket that targets consumers who want to pick up something quickly rather than do a big weekly shop – on the high street and in the petrol fore-court. The table below highlights the development of the supermarkets we see today from the 1980s.

Key events in the supermarket industry since 1987[10]

1987	Argyll buys Safeway's UK arm.
1994	Tesco begins overseas investment programme.
1995	Tesco becomes Britain's largest retailer. J Sainsbury invests £100m to open its first seven stores in Northern Ireland.
1996	Safeway changes its name to Safeway plc.
September 1996	Safeway and oil company BP announce joint retail venture.
February 1997	Tesco opens four of its superstores for all-night shopping on Fridays, becoming the first supermarket chain to offer 24-hour trading outside the Christmas period.
March 1997	Tesco buys Ireland's biggest grocery chain, Power Supermarkets Ltd, from Associated British Foods for £630 million.
May 1997	Marks and Spencer's profits exceed £1 billion.
September 1997	Safeway and Asda suspend merger talks.
19 February 1998	Somerfield and Kwik Save announce plans for a £1.3 billion merger.
July 1998	David Sainsbury steps down as the chairman of J Sainsbury, ending the family's direct control of the company.
October 1998	George Davies signs a three-year, £1-million-per-annum contract with Asda and launches the successful 'George' range of clothing.
March 1999	Safeway drops out of the FTSE 100.
June 1999	Wal-Mart takes over Asda in a £6.7 billion deal.

June 1999	Interbrand estimates Tesco to be the eighth most valuable British brand, worth £1.8 billion.
February 2000	Tesco links with Esso to create Tesco Express at petrol stations.
January 2001	Tesco registers £1 billion in yearly profit.
April 2001	Wm Morrison joins the FTSE-100 for the first time.
July 2001	J Sainsbury announces deal with Boots.
9 January 2003	Wm Morrison announces a £2.9 billion merger deal with Safeway.
13 January 2003	J Sainsbury blocks the Wm Morrison–Safeway merger and is considering a bid for Safeway.
14 January 2003	Wal-Mart joins the battle for Safeway, announcing an all-cash offer.
17 January 2003	US buyout specialist Kohlberg Kravis Roberts confirms approach for Safeway.
20 January 2003	Retail entrepreneur Philip Green considers making a cash offer for Safeway.
12 August 2003	Competition Commission says it needs more time to study bids after last-minute submission by Asda.
18 August 2003	Trade and Industry Secretary Patricia Hewitt receives Competition Commission report into takeover bids.
26 September 2003	Ms Hewitt accepts Commission recommendation to allow Wm Morrison to bid for Safeway. Asda, Tesco and J Sainsbury's bids are blocked.

The graph below shows how this affected grocery market share; Tesco dominates, Sainsbury's is on a decline, Asda (owned by Wal-Mart) grows from strength to strength, and Morrisons is predicted solid growth. The year 2006 predicts only four companies controlling over 95 per cent of the market; this is far from healthy competition.

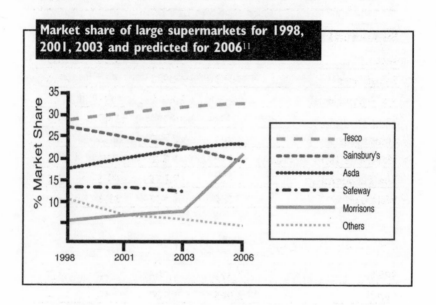

Market share of large supermarkets for 1998, 2001, 2003 and predicted for 2006[11]

Today, supermarkets control over two-thirds of the grocery market and have shares in several others: clothing, books, electronics, petrol, financial services and pharmacy. The list below itemises the 44 companies who sell groceries to the British public, the number of shops, their sales, profits and advertising budgets.

Who Are the Supermarkets?

Retailer	No. of outlets	Sales (£m, excluding sales tax)	Profits (£m)	Advertising (£m)
Leading players in the UK (2000–1)[12]				
Supermarkets				
Tesco	691	18,372	1,054	13.9
Sainsbury's	453	12,931	434	25.6
Wal-Mart (Asda)	240	10,019	405	19.5
Safeway	470	8,151	314.5	1.7
Somerfield	1,904	7,727	-2.6	3.5
Morrisons (Wm Morrison)	110	3,500	219.1	6
The Co-operative	1,623	3,055	45.6	6.1
Waitrose	136	1,982	25.7	3.9
Convenience stores				
SPAR	2,591	1,786	–	1.7
Londis	2,065	1,200	–	–
Costcutter	1,050	936	2.7	–
One Stop	888	655	–	–
Budgens	206	445	17.2	0.9
Mace	745	385	–	–
Farmfoods	242	199	–	2.6
Musgrave	55	180	–	–

Retailer	No. of outlets	Sales (£m, excluding sales tax)	Profits (£m)	Advertising (£m)
Convenience stores (continued)				
Tates	184	172	–	–
EH Booth	24	133	–	–
William Jackson & Son	94	120	–	–
Healds (Day & Nite)	108	116	–	–
Nevins	15	15	–	–
Petrol station convenience stores				
Shell	1,070	662	–	–
BP	1,500	533	–	–
Esso	1,460	480	–	–
TotalFinaElf	1,280	360	–	–
Texaco	1,100	332	–	–
Jet	530	128	–	–
Discount stores				
Kwik Save	734	1,842	-7.2	0.7
ALDI	250	995	-2.2	3.2
Lidl	250	550	–	6.1
Alldays	774	527	–	–
Netto	125	491	–	–

Retailer	No. of outlets	Sales (£m, excluding sales tax)	Profits (£m)	Advertising (£m)
Co-operatives				
United Norwest Co-operatives	454	554	–	–
Midlands Co-operative Society	163	371	–	–
Yorkshire Co-operatives	145	251	–	–
Scottish Midland Co-op	173	196	–	–
Oxford, Swindon & Gloucester Co-op	86	183	–	–
Anglia Regional Co-op	59	170	–	–
Southern Co-op	89	160	–	–
Ipswich & Norwich Co-op	86	158	–	–
Colchester & East Essex Co-op	50	151	–	–
Plymouth & South Devon Co-op	63	138	–	–
Others				
Marks and Spencer (food sales only)	303	2,734	–	–
Iceland	766	2,474	23.2	13.9

The following chart and table show supermarket rankings by sales. Interesting, even though Carrefour is top in Europe and second globally, Wal-Mart has almost four times Carrefour's sales worldwide. Most of the supermarkets listed are truly multinational companies operating across the globe and still expanding.

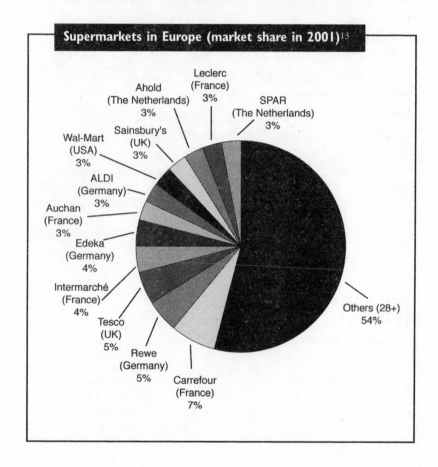

Supermarkets in Europe (market share in 2001)[13]

- Leclerc (France) 3%
- Ahold (The Netherlands) 3%
- SPAR (The Netherlands) 3%
- Wal-Mart (USA) 3%
- Sainsbury's (UK) 3%
- ALDI (Germany) 3%
- Auchan (France) 3%
- Edeka (Germany) 4%
- Intermarché (France) 4%
- Tesco (UK) 5%
- Rewe (Germany) 5%
- Carrefour (France) 7%
- Others (28+) 54%

Top global supermarkets by turnover in 2003[14]

Rank	Company	Top executive	No. of stores	Sales (US $bn)	Countries of operation
1	Wal-Mart Stores (US)	H Lee Scott	5,164	244.5	Arg. Bra. Can. China. Ger. Jap. Mex. Sing. S.Kor. UK US Viet.
2	Carrefour (France)	Daniel Bernard	10,704	64.70	Arg. Belg. Bra. Chile China Col. Cz. Dom. Eg. Fr. Gre. Indon. It. Jap Mal. Mex. Oman, Pol. Port. Qat. Rom. Sing Slova. S. Kor. Sp. Sw. Tai. Thai. Tun. Turk. US
3	Ahold Ltd (Netherlands)	Anders Moberg	9,407	59.20	Arg. Bra. Chile. Costa. Cz. Den. Ecu. El Sal. Est. Guat. Hon. Indon. Lat. Lith. Mex. Neth. Nic. Nor. Par. Peru Pol. Port. Slova. Sp. Swe. Thai. US

Rank	Company	Top executive	No. of stores	Sales (US $bn)	Countries of operation
4	Kroger (US)	Joseph Pichler	3,667	51.80	US
5	Metro (Germany)	Hans-Joachim Korber	2,411	48.50	Austria Belg. Bul. China, Col. Cro. Cz. Den. Fr. Ger. Gre. Hung. India It. Jap. Lux. Mor. Neth. Pol. Port. Rom. Rus. Slova. Sp. Swi. Turk. UK Ukr. Viet.
6	Tesco (UK)	Terry Leahy	2,294	39.50	Cz. Hung. Ire. Mal. Pol. Slova. S.Kor. Tai. Thai. UK US
7	Costco (US)	Jim Sinegal	400	38	Can. Jap. Mex. S.Kor. Tai. UK US
8	Albertsons (US)	Larry Johnston	1,688	35.60	US
9	REWE Zentrale (Germany)	Hans Reischl	12,077	35.20	Austria Bulg. Cro. Cz. Fr. Ger. Hung. It. Pol. Rom. Slov. Ukr.
10	ALDI (Germany)	Theo Albrecht	6,609	33.70	Aus. Austria Belg. Den. Fr. Ger. Ire. Lux. Neth. Sp. UK US

Who Are the Supermarkets?

Rank	Company	Top executive	No. of stores	Sales (US $bn)	Countries of operation
11	Safeway (US)	Steve Burd	1,887	32.40	Can. US
12	ITM Enterprises (France)	Michel Pattou	12,863	31.50	Belg. Bos. Fr. Ger. Pol. Port. Rom. Sp.
13	Ito-Yokado (Japan)	Toshifumi Suzuki	23,700	27.20	Aus. Can. China Jap. Mal. Mex. Phil. Sp. Tai. Thai. Tur. US
14	Edeka (Germany)	Alfons Frenk	14,374	27.00	Aus. Cz. Den. Fr. Ger. Pol.
15	Auchan (France)	Christophe Dubrulle	1,120	25.90	Ang. Arg. China Fr. Hung. It. Lux. Mex. Mor. Pol. Port. Rus. Sp. Tai. US
16	Sainsbury's (UK)	Peter Davis	681	25.90	UK US
17	Aeon (Japan)	Toshiji Tokiwa	8,120	24.60	Can. HK. Jap. S.Kor. Mal. Phil. Thai. UK US
18	Tengelmann (Germany)	Karl-Erivan W Haub	7,015	24.40	Austria Can. China. Cz. Ger. Hung. Pol. Slove. Sp. Swi. US
19	Schwarz Group (Germany)	Gunter Fergen, Klaus Gehrig	5,342	21.60	Austria. Belg. Bul. Cro. Cz. Den. Est. Fin. Fr. Ger. Gre. Hung. Ire. It. Lat. Neth. Nor. Pol. Slov. Sp. Swe. UK

Rank	Company	Top executive	No. of stores	Sales (US $bn)	Countries of operation
20	Casino (France)	Christian Couvreux	9,056	21.50	Arg. Bahr. Belg. Bra. Col. Com. Fr. Leb. Mad. Maur. Mex. Neth. Pol. Tai. Thai. Tun. Ur. US. Ven. Viet.
21	Delhaize Group (Belgium)	Pierre-Olivier Beckers	2,520	19.40	Arg. Bahr. Belg. Bra. Col. Com. Fr. Leb. Mad. Maur. Mex. Neth. Pol. Tai. Thai. Tun. Ur. US Ven. Viet.
22	Leclerc (France)	Michel Leclerc, Edouard Leclerc	535	19.20	Fr. It. Pol. port. Slove. Sp.
23	Supervalu (US)	Jeff Noddle	1,220	19.20	US
24	Daiei (Japan)	Jiro Amagai	4,086	17.70	China Jap. US
25	Publix (US)	Charles Jenkins Jr.	756	15.90	US

KEY

Ang. (Angola), Arg. (Argentina), Aus. (Australia), Austria, Bah. (Bahrain), Belg. (Belgium), Bos. (Bosnia), Bra. (Brazil), Bul. (Bulgaria), Can. (Canada), Chile, China, Col. (Colombia), Costa. (Costa Rica), Com. (Comoros), Cro. (Croatia), Cz. (Czech Republic), Den (Denmark), Dom. (Dominican Republic), Ecu. (Ecuador), Eg. (Egypt), El. (El Salvador), Est. (Estonia), Fin. (Finland), Fr. (France), Ger. (Germany), Gre. (Greece), Guat. (Guatemala), HK. (Hong Kong), Hon. (Honduras), Hung. (Hungary), India, Indon. (Indonesia), Ire. (Ireland), It. (Italy), Jap. (Japan), Leb. (Lebanon), Lat. (Latvia), Lith. (Lithuania), Lux. (Luxembourg), Mad. (Madagascar), Mal. (Malaysia), Maur. (Mauritius), Mex. (Mexico), Mor. (Morocco), Neth. (Netherlands), Nic. (Nicaragua), Nor. (Norway), Oman, Par. (Paraguay), Peru, Phil. (Philippines), Pol. (Poland), Port. (Portugal), Qat. (Qatar), Rom. (Romania), Russia, Sing. (Singapore), Slov. (Slovakia), Slovenia, S. Kor. (S Korea), Sp. (Spain), Swe. (Sweden), Switzerland, Tai. (Taiwan), Thai. (Thailand), Tun. (Tunisia), Turk. (Turkey), UK (United Kingdom), Ukr. (Ukraine), Ur. (Uraguay), US (United States), Ven. (Venezuela), Viet. (Vietnam)

So who are the supermarkets? Where did they come from and how did they develop into the companies we know today?

Tesco

Tesco is the supermarket leader and largest retailer in the UK. It clearly pitches at the middle mass market. Tesco leads the world in online grocery retailing and is the UK's most successful international retailer. It is also a market leader in the Czech Republic, the Slovak Republic, Hungary and Thailand, and has growing businesses in Poland, Korea and Taiwan. In the UK, the company focuses on running grocery superstores (and convenience stores); elsewhere the focus is usually on hypermarkets. [15]

Tesco was founded in 1924 when Sir Jack Cohen started selling groceries in London's East End markets. Supermarket development followed, but the root of its success was the decision led by Ian McLaurin (now Sir Ian) in 1977 to ditch savings stamps and cut prices instead. There followed a major investment in stores and systems, products and own-brand development. The final building block was put in place after the 1990 recession, when the group realised that to compete with the slightly more up-market Sainsbury's it should develop its own clearly defined market position. Tesco was first into the 1990 recession, but also first out, and it has not looked back. It has long had more sales area than Sainsbury's, but its position as market leader was reinforced by the purchase of regional player William Low in 1994.[16]

Having established a strong superstore format financed through the cash flow of numerous small stores (mostly closed down since), Tesco started to innovate. The Metro format was developed for busy city centres, Express for petrol forecourts and Extra as a hypermarket. A refinement of the superstore concept, the Compact store, was developed for smaller catchment areas. Wal-Mart's purchase of Asda subsequently raised the competitive stakes and Tesco has been determined not to lose out, matching and even leading any price cuts to match hypermarket development as well.[17]

Tesco's international expansion, however, got off to a poor start when it missed the opportunity to bid for hypermarket player Docks de France and instead bought family owned chain Catteau in May 1993. Catteau was too small, did not work well and was sold in late 1997. Tesco now has just one store in France; a drinks outlet targeting day-trippers from England. Since then its record has been excellent, and in 2001–2, all countries it had a presence in showed a profit, apart from a start-up operation in Taiwan. In Ireland and Eastern Europe, Tesco tends to make an initial acquisition and then grow through sales; in the Far East the pattern has been to find a local partner and develop through sales.[18]

J Sainsbury

Sainsbury's was number one in the UK from the mid 1980s to mid 1990s, but was beaten by Tesco in 1995, and in 2003 was relegated to number three, its position taken by Asda. If this poor performance continues, it is predicted (see above) to become number four by 2006 behind Morrisons. Its business is based on quality and value for money and is pitched towards the upper end of the middle mass market. The J Sainsbury Group also owns food-retailing businesses under the Shaws name in the US.[19]

The business was founded in 1869 and based on the concepts of quality and a strong own brand. Development of its supermarkets started in the 1950s, and the move outside of its South Eastern heartland came in the 1980s. The business was highly successful and a role model for many other UK retailers, notably Tesco in its 1980s and 1990s recovery phase. From the mid 1980s, when it overtook the Co-op, until the late 1990s when it was overtaken by Tesco, Sainsbury's was the UK market leader. It set the standards in own-brand development and led the way in key areas such as ready-prepared meals.[20]

In 1994 the company's 125th anniversary celebrations were upstaged by Tesco's launch of a loyalty card. This marked the beginning of a loss of momentum, with six years of slowly worsening performance. David Sainsbury had taken over from the team of Sir John Sainsbury and Roy Griffiths, who had led the business through the 1970s and 1980s, and analysts and the media blamed him for the problems. Whatever the reasons, the company appeared to become fixated with profits, stock market rating and saving cash for profits in the short term, and failed to invest sufficiently for the longer term. The stores had begun to look tired, there had been insufficient investment in systems and distribution, marketing was poor and even new-product development seemed to have stalled; it was comprehensively upstaged by the marketing-led recovery at Tesco. Identifying the problems was one thing but, while any success must also owe something to changes made by his predecessors,[21] it was not until Sir Peter Davis was appointed Group Chief Executive in March 2000 that there was any upturn. By the end of the year, like-for-like sales were beginning to recover.

Various attempts to expand into non-foods have not been particularly successful. A chain of hypermarkets was developed under the Savacentre brand, but they never achieved the same returns as a standard Sainsbury's superstore, and in 1999 the management was merged back into the supermarket chain and further development quietly dropped. J Sainsbury also built up the Homebase DIY chain and merged it with Texas to create the number two player in that market. However, in 2000, when the food-retailing activities were under pressure and in need of cash for reinvestment and refurbishment, Homebase was sold to venture capital group Schroder Ventures. In all, after reinvesting £23 million in a 17.8 per cent stake in the business, J Sainsbury realised £952 million.[22]

Expansion outside of the UK started in the 1983 with the acquisition of a stake in Shaws in the US with full control in 1987. The business has been steadily expanded through sales and acquisition since then and is now a significant player in the New England market. A venture in Egypt, started in 1999, was not a success and J Sainsbury engineered an exit at the end of 2000.

Its lack of international development could become a problem; Wal-Mart, Carrefour, Ahold and even Tesco have appreciated the benefits that can come from increased worldwide scale.[23]

Wal-Mart(Asda)

The world's largest retailer – indeed the world's largest company – entered Europe through the acquisition of two chains in Germany and one in the UK (named Asda) in the late 1990s. Since then it has struggled to assimilate and integrate the chains in Germany, although it has built on the existing successes of Asda in the UK to become the UK's number two in 2003. Further European growth is expected, perhaps after recovery in Germany is complete, with moves into France, Switzerland, Spain and Eastern Europe being touted as possible initiatives.[24]

Wal-Mart stems from humble origins with its roots reaching as far back as the 1940s. It was founded by Sam Walton, who began his career in retail as a trainee at JC Penney, the drugstore, department store and catalogue retailer. In 1945 he leased a franchised Ben Franklin store in Newport, Arkansas before relocating to Bentonville, where he opened a Walton 'five-and-dime' (ie cheap) outlet. After Ben Franklin's management rejected Sam Walton's suggestion to open a chain of discount stores in small towns, he (with his brother James 'Bud' Walton) opened the first Wal-Mart Discount City in Rogers, Arkansas in 1962. By 1970, the business was posting sales of $44 million from 18 stores and went public to generate funds for further expansion. Over the next decade, growth was even more rapid than in the previous one, with developments in both the store network and behind-the-scenes infrastructure. Both organic growth and acquisitions continued for that decade, as the store portfolio expanded rapidly across the US, and a number of different formats were developed.[25]

Wal-Mart opened its first Sam's Wholesale Club in 1983, unveiling a warehouse format modelled on Price Company (now better known as Costco). This was followed in 1987 by the opening of Hypermarket USA, a joint venture with Cullum Companies, the Dallas-based supermarket chain. Although not successful in itself, the development of the hypermarket format facilitated the subsequent introduction of what is now the popular Supercenter format; the basis for Wal-Mart's overwhelming domestic domination. The hypermarket featured over 18,600 square metres of sales area in an environment reminiscent of a shopping centre, including complementary businesses such as banks, fast-food outlets and pharmacies. In July 1998 Wal-Mart unveiled the Neighborhood Market format; 3,700-square-metre units intended to serve the needs of urban markets or those located between Supercenter sites.[26]

Wal-Mart's global spread commenced in 1992 via a joint venture with Mexico's largest retailer, Cifra. The group entered Puerto Rico in 1993 and in 1994 moved northwards into Canada with the acquisition of 122 former Woolco stores from Woolworth Canada. The next couple of years saw entry into the Brazilian,

Argentinean and Chinese markets before the first move into Europe in 1997 with the acquisition of 21 Wertkauf hypermarkets. After acquiring several stores and undeveloped sites in South Korea in early 1998, Wal-Mart consolidated its position in Germany with the acquisition of 74 INTERSPAR hypermarkets. This was followed by the July 1999 takeover of Asda, which was trading from 229 outlets at the time. Subsequent moves have included entry into Japan via a 6.1 per cent stake in ailing Japanese business Seiyu. Speculation continues unabated, however, with a number of other businesses, particularly in France and Spain, being cited as possible targets.[27]

Wm Morrison/Safeway

Until its recent merger, Safeway was the fourth largest and historically the weakest of the big four food retailers in the UK, although it staged an impressive revival under Chief Executive Carlos Criado-Perez. It has no branches outside of the UK.

Two businesses led the rationalisation of the UK food-retailing industry in the 1980s; Safeway and Somerfield Groups. What was to become Safeway Stores had the much happier and more successful history, as developed by James Gulliver, Alistair Grant and David Webster with the acquisition of Oriel Foods in 1972. Several more purchases followed and the company decided to focus on the Presto name. But in February 1987 the group bought Safeway UK from its US parent in a deal worth £681 million. Safeway was a far stronger business in terms of operating style, customer trust and brand strength. The group soon decided to focus on the Safeway brand, first in a two-tier portfolio with Presto used for smaller stores, but eventually branding all stores Safeway, and in 1996 adopting the Safeway name for the group.[28]

Safeway's weaknesses stemmed from being fourth on the scene in a market dominated by three clearly defined strong players. Although it had, like Tesco and Sainsbury's, used the cash flow from less economic small stores to fund expansion of larger outlets, its stores tended to be smaller and not as well sited as the majors. The business was successful but lagged behind the leaders particularly in terms of fresh food development. It also struggled to develop a clear identity; even when it focused on families, backed by a highly successful television advertising campaign featuring a small boy, it still tended to live in the shadow of Sainsbury's. All too often Safeway's efforts looked like 'me-toos'.

Before merging with Safeway, Wm Morrison was a chain of 114 supermarkets based mainly in the north of England, where it competes head-on with Asda. The company experienced difficulty in finding suitable sites in the south of England, until it merged with Safeway, becoming number three in the UK. The Morrison family retains a 38 per cent stake in the business.

Somerfield

As the fifth and weakest of the major UK food retailers, Somerfield weakened its position further by taking on Kwik Save, the ailing 'soft' discounter (selling a wide range of products at low prices) in 1998. The stores are generally too large to be convenience shops and too small to be full-line supermarkets. Somerfield has no interests outside of the UK. Both Somerfield and Safeway are the result of a series of acquisitions in the 1980s. But where Safeway forged a strong new business, the Dee Corporation – later to become Somerfield – was unable to solve the retail problems of its unwieldy group. Operating everything from former Carrefour outlets to small corner shops, Dee decided to focus on a single trading name, Gateway. In 1989 the business was the victim of a management buy-in and break-up. Asda took the larger stores; the rump was left to the buy-in vehicle Isosceles. This new business struggled, hampered by far too much debt, and experimented with several different names and formats. It was not until a new team led by David Simons took over in 1992 and focused on one name and one trading format, Somerfield, that the business began to move forward.[29]

Kwik Save was at that time the biggest and most successful discounter in the UK. But it was wrong footed by German-based, 'hard' discounter ALDI's decision to enter the UK market. Faced with the choice between competing head on with ALDI or trying to differentiate itself, Kwik Save chose the latter route; but that meant competing with the superstores, a battle it was totally ill equipped to fight, not having adequate systems or fresh food expertise. By February 1998, when Somerfield stepped in with a rescue bid, Kwik Save's performance was entering into free fall. Somerfield tried to convert all the stores to its own format, and then attempted to sell those that were unsuitable; only in 2000 did it decide to continue to run the Kwik Save fascia as an independent entity. The larger Somerfield stores and about half of the Kwik Save chain were put up for sale. The former found ready buyers; the latter did not. Then, in March 2000, David Simons left. He was replaced by John von Spreckelson as executive and Alan Smith as managing director. They halted the sale programme and salvaged any existing Kwik Saves. Since then the performance has certainly improved, even though the group is still losing market share. John von Spreckelsen had an excellent record at Budgens and has City backing.[30] So the business has some breathing space but could well struggle again with the impact of the Morrisons merger, effectively relegating Somerfield to a minor supermarket player.

The Co-operative Group

The UK's two leading co-operative societies, Co-operative Wholesales Society Ltd (CWS) and Co-operative Retail Services Ltd (CRS), merged in 2000 to create a retail group that now has 1,100 stores. There was very little overlap in trading area between the two groups, which both focus on the convenience/small supermarket end of the grocery retail sector in urban and rural communities. The Co-operative Group also includes other businesses; non-food, Funeralcare and Travelcare, which are managed by the Commercial Division, and the Priory Motor Group, which is separately managed by the North Eastern & Cumbrian Region.[31]

Marks and Spencer

Marks and Spencer (M&S) was founded in Leeds in 1884, went public in 1926 and built its name and reputation on its quality, value and service. M&S is Europe's leading retailer of clothing, although it long since diversified into other product areas, of which food is the most important. Its clothing targets the upper-to-middle end of the mass market and both areas are designed to appeal to a broad spectrum of consumers. There are now 362 M&S stores in the UK, including 3 franchised stores in the Channel Islands, plus 18 Simply Food stores, including 4 franchised units. Internationally, directly run operations now comprise 4 stores in the Republic of Ireland, 10 in Hong Kong and the 27-store Kings Super Markets business in the US. There are also 80 franchised M&S stores worldwide. The last five years has been a turbulent period for M&S, after a sharp fall in sales and profits at the end of the 1990s that plunged the business into crisis. In March 2001, under a new management team, M&S announced a sweeping restructuring, including the disposal of most of its directly owned international interests. Two years on, strong growth in both sales and profits suggest that it has responded to the challenge well.[32]

Iceland

Iceland is a leading grocery retailer in the frozen foods market and a publicly quoted company. The company merged with cash and carry giant Booker in June 2000, aiming to create a larger group that could serve both retail and trade customers, giving Iceland much greater buying power in areas such as ambient grocery, wines, spirits and soft drinks, and providing Booker with a much stronger frozen range. Booker serves more than 100,000 independent retailers through a national network of over 180 cash-and-carry depot outlets. The enlarged Iceland group changed its name in February 2002 to The Big Food Group plc to reflect its new status as an integrated food provider. However, Iceland and Booker continue to trade under their own names.[33]

Waitrose

Waitrose is part of the John Lewis Partnership that reflects the principle 'never knowingly undersold'. Waitrose operates in a very different way to other grocery multiples: every permanent employee is a 'partner' in the company and shares in the profits, as well as having a say in the running of the business. Waitrose occupies a premium position in the grocery market and appeals to an up-market, middle-class customer base. The company had 136 branches at the end of 2001, reflecting a steady expansion of the chain.[34]

Londis

Londis is the fastest-growing symbol group – where independent retailers pay a marketing/promotion company for the right to use its name over their shop – in the UK, with around 2,000 franchise members, all of whom are independent retailers. Londis provides its members with bulk-buying benefits as well as access to marketing, store development, technology and retail expertise. It offers a range of over 4,000 lines, and delivers goods to the shop premises from Londis distribution centres. Additionally, over 200 leading suppliers deliver goods direct to stores, giving retailers a choice of lines.[35]

ALDI

ALDI was the pioneering developer of the hard-discount formula and has since exported its successful concept across the globe. It is the world's leading hard discounter, trading from around 5,900 stores in Europe, the US and Australia. The Aldi-Gruppe is divided into two independent companies: ALDI Nord, which trades in Germany, Belgium, Denmark, France, Luxembourg and the Netherlands; and ALDI Sud, which trades in Germany, Austria, the UK, Ireland, the US and Australia. The virtual saturation of the German market has forced ALDI to look towards other countries for opportunities, and its highly transportable retail format has allowed it to take advantage of opportunities in other markets. The definitive ALDI concept was formulated in this period; limited ranges of products sold at low prices in basic, no-frills stores with few staff. This model prevails today.

Germany is by far the largest market for ALDI, but competition in the shape of Lidl, Penny (REWE), Edeka, Plus (Tengelmann), Norma and Netto has forced ALDI to look elsewhere for growth opportunities. Following a late-1960s move into next-door Austria, the real cross-border shift commenced in the 1970s, when the group entered the Dutch, Danish and Belgian markets. The business subsequently opened in France, the UK, the US and Luxembourg, with entry into Ireland and Australia following in 1999/2000. Store openings in Spain are currently being prepared, while Turkey is also thought to be under evaluation.[36]

SPAR International

Claiming to be 'the world's largest retail food store chain', SPAR International is a marketing and buying organisation that oversees the activities of independent and multiple food retailers in 29 countries across the world. It is present in 22 European markets, with 11,000 shops operated by 2,000 independent retailers. Adriaan van Well, who decided that a co-operation of independent retailers and wholesalers would be of strong mutual benefit, founded SPAR in the Netherlands in 1932. The SPAR system was duplicated in different countries over the years until 2002, with its fascia now used in 29 countries. Each national unit operates as a separate entity, with the SPAR International operation serving as an advisory and marketing body. It has no powers over its national members; instead making recommendations and suggestions to them. Some central buying is undertaken (including both resalable and non-resalable products) and its BIGS buying department has developed the SPAR own-brand.[37]

Netto

Netto is part of Dansk Supermarked, which is owned by MAERSK and F Salling A/S. In the UK it is a chain of local discount grocery stores based mainly in central and northern England in large industrial cities in such as Sheffield, Manchester and Newcastle. It caters for customers from lower income groups.[38]

Budgens

Budgens is a publicly quoted company that operates a chain of neighbourhood supermarkets. The Irish grocery retailer the Musgrave Group currently holds a 44 per cent interest in the company.[39]

Lidl

Although best known for its Lidl hard-discount chain, the Schwarz holding company also comprises the Kaufland and KaufMarkt hypermarket division and Handelshof and Concord food retailing superstores. Other activities include DIY stores, food wholesale, manufacturing and food service. The German market still accounts for the bulk of sales, despite extremely vigorous expansion of the hard discount formula in other European markets.

The focus of growth has been the Lidl chain, which has been exported throughout Western Europe. Lidl is now concentrating on new markets in Eastern Europe and Scandinavia, and the Kaufland hypermarket format has also been opened in Central and Eastern European markets. The domestic superstore/hypermarket chain was boosted in 2000 when Schwarz, Dohle and Bartels-Langness divided Tengelmann's Grosso-Magnet superstore division between them. As already noted, foreign expansion has very much been at the forefront of Schwarz' agenda over the last decade, with well over 15 new markets seeing Lidl and Kaufland stores open since the late 1980s. Further expansion into Eastern and Central Europe is being investigated, and Scandinavia is also a keen area of interest.[40]

The verdict

The supermarkets we see today have become incredibly successful businesses providing products and a format that consumers worldwide like. The top 25 supermarkets globally (shown on the table, page 13) demonstrate that it is the European and US companies that have perfected the supermarket format and are now relentlessly marching into Eastern Europe and Asia. The origins and format vary, but what is clear is that over the last 30 years they have become a large part of the consumer's life.

Now that the power of the top UK supermarkets – in terms of sheer size and control of the food we buy – has been laid bare, it is time to turn to the impact these supermarkets have on our world. This incredible power in the marketplace is the basis for the argument that supermarkets are responsible for social and environmental damage far beyond these brightly lit 'super shops'.

Chapter 2

Suppliers and Farmers

*They [supermarkets] love to come over as
marvellous people ... that they are all squeaky
clean and it's all hunkydory and it's all nice.
But some of the stories of the way people are
treated, it's horrendous. They [supermarkets]
do use this situation, that they are very big
and we are a lot of small suppliers. What can
we do up against them? The history of farmers
creating co-operatives to try and match their
powers has been basically a failure. We've been
down that route through the NFU [National
Farmers Union] of saying to government; why
not do as what other industries do and have a
watchdog and an ombudsman? They will not
have that at all. Government do not want to
really know, they know food is cheap and
that's what the public wants. They know very
well that if they went down the line of an
ombudsman the food would go much dearer.
We feel, as an industry, we are being taken
for a ride.*

Welsh Dairy and Livestock Farmer, 25/01/04

By far the biggest impact of supermarkets is on suppliers,
particularly farmers. Supermarkets, especially the big

four – Tesco, Asda, Sainsbury's and Morrisons/Safeway – constantly squeeze the price of products, while at the same time making huge profits. Some argue that the process of increasing wealth in society depends on reducing costs – figuring out ways to do something quicker, cheaper and faster – to push down prices. This is tough on the individuals and businesses that have to find ways of cutting costs, but society as a whole benefits.[1] However, this is naive economic logic that ignores the fact that society comprises more than just supermarkets and consumers. Many suppliers are forced out of business because there are no alternative buyers, with supermarkets having a monopoly over markets.

There have recently been two intensive government inquiries into the supermarket industry, documenting the devastating impact of supermarkets on suppliers. The farming industry, small regional producers and large branded-product manufacturers have called the supermarkets bullies for a long time; the question is why the UK government still refuses to intervene, and why consumers have failed to demand that supermarkets treat farmers and suppliers fairly.

This chapter will explain the supermarkets' process of trading with farmers and suppliers and the bullying tactics they use. The reality of the relationship is laid bare, along with the consequences on farming, the attempt at a voluntary code of practice and the results of the recent supermarket 'merger fever'.

How suppliers trade with supermarkets

Over the course of the 20th century, market dominance by distributors and wholesalers gave way to dominance by manufacturers, followed by supermarkets. The food-service sector, including fast food, is also increasing in importance and is expected to grow from a current 30 per cent of consumer spending on food to 50 per cent by 2020.[2]

Supermarkets depend on their suppliers to provide the products that they sell, at the right time, in the right quantity, of appropriate quality and at a competitive price. Both supermarkets and suppliers stress that it is vital that their relationship works well. But they have different objectives; suppliers want to sell at the highest price they can and supermarkets want to buy at the lowest costs, so some tension is inevitable.[3]

The table below shows how supermarkets make use of suppliers, from 2,535 suppliers for Sainsbury's to 4,471 for Morrisons, with Sainsbury's getting 87 per cent of its products from grocery suppliers compared to 37 per cent for Morrisons. This highlights, not surprisingly, the fact that supermarkets selling only groceries have fewer suppliers than retailers who sell a wide range of products. On the other hand, the number of suppliers does not relate to the size of the supermarket or how many different products it sells. The surprising figures are the numbers of products – ranging from around 13,000 to 18,000 – available for consumers, which shows that if you cannot find what you want, you are not looking hard enough!

Number of suppliers and products sold[4]

Retailer	Total suppliers	% of goods from grocery suppliers	No. of products
Asda	3,921	49	12,994
Morrisons	4,471	37	17,090
Safeway	2,684	69	17,671
Sainsbury's	2,535	87	17,671
Tesco	3,677	61	18,261

Suppliers range from large multinational conglomerates, with worldwide sales of over £25 billion, through national groups to specialist cottage-industry providers with sales of under £1 million.[5] Around one-fifth of supplies to the supermarkets are imported.

The UK government's Competition Commission provides further insight into relations between supermarkets and their suppliers. The Commission has conducted two major inquiries, one on supermarket monopolies in 2000 and one on the takeover of Safeway in 2003. Many suppliers manufacture products to retailers' own specifications, which are sold on under a retailer's own-label brand (exclusively or in addition to the supplier's brand).[6] While outside Europe own-label products typically account for less than 5 per cent of total food sales, in Europe they make up 45 per cent.[7] For some of the UK supermarkets, own-label products represent a sizeable proportion of the goods they sell, with the supermarket owning the intellectual property rights (patents and copyrights).[8]

Suppliers of branded goods, of course, want wide distribution for their products and generally seek to trade with all supermarkets (unlike most suppliers of fresh fruit and vegetables, meat, poultry and some supermarkets' own-label chilled products, who appear to concentrate on trade with a limited number – often four or less – of the supermarkets). Many manufacturers of branded goods also supply supermarkets' own-label products, which compete with their own-branded products. Others specialise in supermarkets' own-label products and either do not produce branded goods, or produce only 'secondary' or 'tertiary' branded products, ie cheap, minor brands selling at lower prices than premium brands.[9]

So supermarkets depend on suppliers for all the goods they sell; and suppliers, in theory, have the option of selling to retailers other than the supermarkets. In practice, however, most suppliers sell the majority of their output to the supermarkets. For example, the largest four supermarkets – Tesco, Asda, Sainsbury's and Morrisons/Safeway – account for over 70 per cent of the UK sales of the two major competing brands of washing powder, Persil and Ariel. Many smaller suppliers are dependent on a single supermarket for all their sales.[10]

Supermarket buyers

Supermarket buyers tend to operate at corporate or head-office level, with few store managers purchasing locally. In Europe just 110 'buying desks', made up of a team of buyers from a supermarket, act as gatekeepers between 3.2 million farmers and 250 million consumers; retailers are the funnel point and declining in numbers.[11] While buyers may be in regular contact with suppliers for a time (both supermarkets and suppliers cite continuity as vital for maintaining healthy relationships), their career paths result in them moving around to cover different product ranges, sometimes as frequently as every two years.[12] A small supplier commented to the Competition Commission in its supermarket inquiry in 2000 that:

> *The power of the multiples, and especially of young (c.25–28) buyers, without experience, is frightening. [They have] the power to dictate prices and margins, display or not, allocate space and threaten covertly. It's why we would never allow more than 15 per cent of turnover to be supplied to multiples.[13]*

Suppliers' organisations were often more willing to speak at the Competition Commission's inquiry than small suppliers. One commented that the big supermarkets:

> *. . . talk about partnerships, but these do not exist, and they ruthlessly erode suppliers' margins with no consideration of the damage they are doing to that company or its employees. Multiples switch their buyers around every six to twelve months in order that relationships and loyalty to suppliers*

can be avoided. The new buyer is given carte blanche to delist suppliers, who are frequently treated with complete contempt.[14]

And another maintained that:

… many of our individual members are extremely reluctant, or refuse point blank, to comment on specific cases. Many of these organisations have 40, 50, 60 or even 70 per cent of their sales with a multiple. The resultant power that the multiples have is huge. This power is often rested in the hands of a small buying team, often young, who are changed at short notice routinely. This makes it extremely difficult to maintain stability within the industry.[15]

The power of this small number of young buyers is exacerbated by the authorised bullying tactics they use against suppliers.

Bullying practices

The International Institute for Environment and Development, which ranks supermarkets, has concluded that supermarkets achieve 'economies of scale' (ie lower costs as a result of their size) partly through bringing buying power to bear on suppliers, capping farm prices against retailers' precise gross margins by the use of direct contracting, rather than suppliers competing on price, and by the use of (or threat of) imports. Farmers and growers say that they are left with 'take it or leave it' deals. The system of no contracts preferred by supermarkets and their first-tier suppliers for sourcing own-label produce are now such a large part of the livestock and produce industries that there is no competitive market (eg live auctions) where real market prices can be 'discovered'. The wholesale market represents the price of residual production (and lower quality production) surplus to supermarket requirements; farmers who supply wholesale markets, especially in marginal areas, are the most economically endangered sector of UK agriculture.[16]

During the Competition Commission inquiries, most suppliers were unwilling to be named or to name the subject of the allegation. It reported that there appeared to be a climate of apprehension among many suppliers in their relationship with supermarkets. In the Commission's 2000 report it listed 52 alleged practices against suppliers during 1995–2000; the large supermarkets admitted to engaging in the majority of these practices,[17] including:[18]

1. **Requiring suppliers to make payments or concessions to gain access to supermarket shelf space.**

2. **Imposing conditions relating to suppliers' trade with other retailers.**

3. Applying different standards to different suppliers' offers.

4. Imposing an unfair imbalance of risk.

5. Imposing retrospective changes to contractual terms with suppliers.

6. Restricting suppliers' access to the market.

7. Imposing charges and transferring costs to suppliers.

8. Requiring suppliers of groceries to use third-party suppliers, such as packaging companies, nominated by a supermarket.

The Competition Commission states that these practices, when carried out by any of the major supermarkets – Asda, Safeway, Sainsbury's, Somerfield and Tesco – adversely affect the competitiveness of some of their suppliers, with some likely to invest less and spend less on new-product development and innovation, leading to lower quality and less consumer choice. Certain practices give the major buyers substantial advantages over smaller retailers, whose competitiveness is likely to suffer as a result, again leading to a reduction in consumer choice.[19] The chart below details 30 practices that the Commission found were used against suppliers; it is interesting to note that out of the 30 practices both Asda and Safeway used 21, Somerfield 16, Sainsbury's 12 and Tesco 10.

Practices engaged in by any of the major buyers showing findings on the complex monopoly situation and the public interest [20]

Supermarket	Practice
Safeway Somerfield	Required or requested payments from suppliers as a condition of stocking and displaying their products, or as a pre-condition for being on supermarkets' list of suppliers.
Asda Safeway	Required or requested suppliers to make a payment for better positioning of their products within stores.
Safeway Sainsbury's Somerfield Tesco	Required or requested that suppliers give an improvement in terms of return for increasing the range/depth of distribution of their products within the stores.
Asda Safeway Sainsbury's Tesco	Required or requested a financial contribution from a supplier in return for its products being promoted within the store during the year.
Safeway	Required suppliers to give overriding or 'in anticipation' discounts.
Asda Safeway Sainsbury's Somerfield	Sought discounts from suppliers retrospectively that reduced the price of the product agreed at the time of sale.
Asda Safeway Somerfield	Required or requested compensation from a supplier when profits from a product were less than expected.
Asda Safeway Sainsbury's Somerfield	Sought support from a supplier to match a lower retail price of a product by a competing retailer.

Supermarket Practice

Asda Safeway Sainsbury's Somerfield Tesco	Required or requested suppliers to make payments to cover product wastage.
Asda Safeway Somerfield	Required or requested suppliers to buy back unsold items, or failed to pay for them outside a written agreement that 'sale or return' was in the terms of the sale.
Asda Safeway Sainsbury's Somerfield Tesco	Required or requested suppliers to contribute to costs of buyer visits to new or prospective suppliers, artwork and packaging design, consumer panels, market research, or to provide hospitality to the supermarket's employees.
Asda Safeway Sainsbury's	Failed to compensate suppliers for costs caused through the supermarket's forecasting errors or order changes.
Sainsbury's	Levied charges on suppliers for consumer complaints that exceeded actual costs, or were not for a product fault, or for which written information was not provided to the supplier.
Safeway	Required or requested suppliers to contribute specifically to the costs of store refurbishment or the opening of a new store.
Asda Safeway	Introduced a change to any aspect of the supply chain procedures that could reasonably be expected to increase a supplier's costs without compensating the supplier or sharing any savings achieved.
Asda Safeway	Delayed payments to suppliers outside agreed contractual periods, or by more than 30 days from the date of invoice, where deliveries had been made to the supermarket's specification.

Supermarket Practice

Asda Sainsbury's Safeway Somerfield Tesco	Discriminated between suppliers in the length of credit period accepted.
Asda Somerfield	Changed the quantities or specifications of a product previously agreed with a supplier with less than 3 days' notice without financially compensating the supplier for any losses incurred.
Asda Safeway Sainsbury's Somerfield Tesco	Required suppliers to purchase goods or services from designated companies, eg hauliers, packaging companies, labelling companies.
Asda	Required suppliers to maintain a lower wholesale price previously renegotiated for an increased order when the volumes purchased were subsequently reduced.
Asda Safeway	Over-ordered goods at a promotional price from a supplier, which were subsequently sold into retail at a higher price without compensating the supplier.
Asda Somerfield	Sold a product on which the labelling indicated, or might be taken to indicate, that the product was of UK/British origin when the consumable originated overseas (eg when it was packed in the UK after being imported from abroad).
Tesco	Predominantly required suppliers to fund the cost of promotions such as 'Buy one, get one free'.

Supermarket Practice

Asda Safeway	Instigated a promotion on a product without the agreement of the supplier and requested the supplier retrospectively to fund the promotion.
Asda Tesco	Required or requested suppliers to permanently reduce the previously agreed wholesale price of products in support of the marketing initiatives within which the price was initially associated.
Asda Somerfield	Required or requested suppliers to make a financial contribution if a promotional activity carried out by the supermarket failed to meet expected target.
Somerfield	Required supplier to bear the cost of surplus special packaging ordered by the supermarket for a promotion when sales did not meet expectations.
Safeway Sainsbury's Somerfield Tesco	Required or requested suppliers to make a financial contribution to the costs of barcode changes or reduced-price-marked packs.
Asda Safeway Sainsbury's Somerfield Tesco	Invited suppliers to make contributions to charitable organisations (directly or by participation in events designed to raise money for such bodies).
Somerfield	Required or requested suppliers to make payments for a specific promotion (eg gondola ends, advertising allowances) where the payments exceeded the actual costs to the company.

Examples of bullying

One supplier told the Competition Commission that over a period of several months it had been asked by one supermarket to make three separate cash contributions; the third was for a sum in excess of £100,000 for 'a contribution towards profits'. The supplier said that the same supermarket had introduced other charges, none of which had been negotiated and all of which had been deducted from the next payment. There had been no recourse to complain for fear of 'upsetting the relationship'. The supplier added that it had been directed by the supermarket to use a specified freight company, even if this meant breaking an existing contract with another company.[21]

The Commission challenged Tesco on four specific complaints concerning practices for which it had found documentary evidence:[22]

(a) A suppliers' representative body had a letter from Tesco sent to a pack house instructing them that produce from two growers (who had previously supplied Tesco) was no longer to be used. Failure would result in immediate suspension of the pack house's business with Tesco. The suppliers' representative body stated that the produce had become scarce a couple of weeks earlier because of cold weather: the growers had told their packer that they could not supply him because the price he was offering was too low. Tesco's response was that its buyer had decided that the quality of produce from the two former growers was inadequate and that they were no longer going to supply Tesco. Concerned that the quality going into that pack house for other retailers might find its way into Tesco's supply chain, the buyer had instructed the pack house not to take produce from these growers. Tesco said that the buyer had no intention of depriving other retailers of stock but was attempting to ensure that products from a supplier with which he had ceased trading did not enter Tesco's order. As this represented a departure from company policy, the buyer concerned had been reprimanded.

(b) A general store in Tredegar had begun undercutting an adjacent Tesco store on the price of bread, supplied to both outlets by a local bakery. The Tesco store manager had allegedly threatened to cancel their contract with the bakery if it did not persuade the general store to increase its price. The general store has since ceased trading. Tesco said it appeared that, following customer complaints, the store manager had spoken directly to the bakery regarding this price differential. The bakery subsequently contacted Tesco's buying manager to clarify the situation, who assured the supplier that it would continue to carry its products and would in no way attempt to dictate its trading terms with other retailers. Tesco added that the store manager in Tredegar at that time was no longer in its employment. It said that it took such complaints seriously. Such behaviour would be against company policy and practice and, therefore, unlikely to happen.

(c) A letter from a Tesco supermarket to its suppliers stated that there were too many invoice queries due to suppliers not invoicing at the correct case cost. It said that if these queries continued after suppliers had been contacted, an administration charge – £1,000 for the same query two weeks running, and £1,000 for every week thereafter until resolved – would be raised to cover the costs incurred within Tesco. Tesco said that the letter was a notification of a proposed administrative charge in the event of persistent invoice errors. No such charge had actually been deducted from any supplier. Suppliers were warned by Tesco of its intention to seek compensation for specific errors or omissions. The suppliers then had the opportunity to enter into discussions about the reasons for and levels of such payments.

(d) Muskaan Limited, a small supplier of ethnic foods, now in receivership, said that one of Tesco's 'category managers' (responsible for analysing data on consumer preferences) had written to it about a price-marking problem on an item supplied in the Republic of Ireland. Tesco would impose fines of £10,000 per product 'in order to focus your business on getting deliveries right in the first place'. Tesco said that suppliers knew the parameters within which deductions for errors or omissions by suppliers were made. It said that where errors had occurred, suppliers had been warned of Tesco's intention to seek compensation. Tesco confirmed that letters of the same sort had been sent to suppliers of groceries in the UK.

Finally, in November 1999, Safeway, attempting to improve availability of key products, decided to guarantee the availability of 1,000 of its most popular lines. It wrote to the relevant suppliers asking for a payment of £20,000 per line to help finance investment in store wages, stock-holding and wastage costs. For suppliers of more than one line, the contributions sought were extremely large, and for small businesses depending on contracts with one or two retailers for their viability, the impact would be devastating. Safeway stated that, if sales growth projections were achieved, its suppliers would get a healthy return on this investment very quickly. Where several suppliers supplied a product line the contribution Safeway was seeking from each was far less than £20,000 and was being resolved by negotiation. Safeway added that there was no question of this scheme being imposed on anyone; it was a voluntary scheme. If any supplier felt he could not support the scheme, Safeway would withdraw this product and no penalty of any kind would be imposed.[23]

No contracts

Full written agreements between the supermarkets and their suppliers are unusual, with day-to-day negotiations (particularly on price and quantity) usually conducted verbally. Some of the larger supermarkets told the Competitions Commission that full written agreements are not generally applicable in this industry; the large numbers made detailed individual legal contracts impractical. With computerised, sales-based ordering, Tesco said that the relationship with its suppliers is about a constant series of interactions, with volumes and delivery dates being confirmed electronically. Safeway said it does not accept any adverse effects arising from its conduct towards suppliers, but acknowledged that there were concerns, especially among smaller suppliers, regarding their relationships with supermarkets. For some of the supermarkets, standard terms and conditions – covering routine legal issues such as insurance, title to goods and risk – were in place, but specific terms for individual suppliers, which depended on the nature of the product (covering quality, volume, specification, delivery date or price) were often verbal. Suppliers supported these statements and suggested that moving towards written contracts might assist them.[24]

Copycat products

Some suppliers suggested to the Commission that the supermarkets used branded manufacturers, both large and small, as a source of innovation for new products, which they then copied. New ideas are given trial listings, normally in a few stores, and if a trial was successful, some supermarkets launch their own-label imitation of the product at lower prices, often using almost identical packaging and recipes. This inevitably resulted in lost sales for the original brand, at worst resulting in 'delisting', or being removed from a supermarket's preferred suppliers list. [25]

Category management

Category management entails a leading supplier being responsible for analysing data on consumer preferences; identifying the best means of meeting them; determining the most effective ways in which suppliers can provide the relevant products, in terms of range and allocation of space; and advising the supermarket accordingly.

Some suppliers are concerned about category management. Firstly, category managers may give privileged access to sales data of one supplier, compared with its competitors. Secondly, only the very largest suppliers have sufficient resources to participate in projects simultaneously with all their major customers, giving them a potentially significant advantage. Some smaller suppliers are concerned that category management, and consequent consolidation practices by the supermarkets, result in them losing business and could also act as a barrier to entry, especially for secondary and tertiary brands. A trade association commented to the Commission that, when a category manager was appointed, this was predictably the brand leader in that category.[26] It added:

> *This mitigates heavily against smaller suppliers and the strong regional brand as unfair priority is given to new entrants to the market, with regionality being streamed out.*[27]

A number of smaller suppliers believed that category management favoured larger suppliers:

> *Category management will normally favour the larger, often multinational, companies and brands due to their greater resources and negotiating strength;* [28]

> **The UK brand leader in cakes is allowed to control the cake section;** [29]

and

> *. . . category management benefits the larger supplier who specifically dominates the category at the expense of smaller suppliers.*[30]

Another supplier referred to the 'delisting' of some products as multiples moved all similar lines to a category manager.[31]

Pricing and discounts

Complaints to the Competition Commission by suppliers (especially those supplying fresh produce, meat products, dairy and bakery products) included the (in their view unreasonably) low prices for their goods.

Some suppliers suggested that this was exacerbated by new procedures or regulations where the supermarkets improved their own efficiency at the supplier's cost. Many complained that they were forced to participate in the supermarkets' promotions of particular products, under the threat of delisting. This meant selling at a lower price or even at a loss.[32]

Below-cost selling

Tesco was found to pay the lowest prices to their suppliers. In 2000, Tesco introduced international 'reverse' auctions for its suppliers; food suppliers from all over the world are asked to bid to undercut each other until Tesco gets the lowest price. Farmers and other suppliers are put under enormous pressure to cut their prices, even below the break-even point, or lose their market.[33] As a result, farmers are frequently paid less than the cost of production for their goods. A National Farmers Union survey in September 2002 found that for a basket of food (beef, eggs, milk, bread, tomatoes and apples) that would cost £37 in the supermarkets, the farmers would only get £11.26. A Friends of the Earth survey of supermarket apples further revealed that there was a significant mark-up on the 'farm-gate' price (ie amount paid to the farmer or grower).[34]

Suppliers are concerned that below-cost selling could distort the price structure of whole-product groups (such as chocolate), and hence the mix of products consumers buy. They are also worried that it puts enormous pressure on manufacturers to reduce prices to offset retailers' losses as consumers switch to products sold below cost.[35] One supplier told the Competition Commission that:

> *The retailers can absorb the losses because of sales mix, many manufacturers cannot.*[36]

For example, the cheapest baked beans on display were originally sold at 16p to 19p and accounted for 13 per cent of the market. The price subsequently fell to 9p and sales then accounted for 37 per cent of volume. During the so-called 'baked bean wars' period, prices fell to 3p–5p per can.[37] Nestlé closed its Crosse & Blackwell canning operations and withdrew from that area of business, telling the Competition Commission that:

> *. . . we literally could not can fresh air for the price they wanted to retail it at . . . the cans were costing us more than [that]'.*[38]

The effects of below-cost selling in the UK vegetable canning industry were exacerbated by adverse exchange rates. In addition, some overseas companies were willing to trade at prices below normally commercially viable levels in an effort to fill spare capacity. As Nestlé closed all its UK canning operations in 1998, another supplier imported all its canned vegetables. In another example, bakeries are concerned about the supermarkets' use of the standard sliced white loaf as a 'loss leader' (ie leading sales but making a loss) by typically retailing at 9p a loaf, creating a belief among customers that other types of bread are overpriced.[39]

On the positive side, although the supermarkets were accused by some of making profits from farmers during the BSE crisis, the Competition Commission found no evidence for this. It found that the costs in the supply chain rose significantly and the price for farm animals fell because of the reduced price of some of the by-products. At the same time, consumer demand for beef and lamb fell, making it impossible for retailers to raise prices. There was also little dispute that farmers felt the bulk of the effect of higher costs and lower value. Unfortunately, this is the outcome of what the Commission calls a 'broadly competitive market'. Unless retailers had previously been making excessive profits on fresh meat, they would only have been able to pay producers more by reducing their own margins. On the other hand, the Commission found suppliers of retailers' own-label bread, lettuce, apples, eggs, lamb and chicken, to be selling these products by and large at a loss.[40] If the Competition Commission is happy with this type of 'competitive market', there is a serious risk that many suppliers will go bankrupt and the knock-on effect will be that we will lose the diversity and range of products available to the consumer.

Farm-gate verses supermarket prices

With over three-quarters of the UK grocery market in the hands of supermarkets, it is not surprising that the finger of blame for the crisis in UK farming has shifted from government to the big supermarkets. According to the International Institute for Environment and Development (IIED), a majority of farmers feel marginalised by the collapse in the wholesale market, a lack of alternative markets, the selling of goods below cost of production, and a widening gap between 'farm-gate' price (ie the price farmers sell for) and retail price (the price at the till). There is a suspicion among UK farmers that supermarkets are earning too much of their margin from suppliers (through charging for shelf space, charges for listing new products etc) rather than from earning it off consumers. Aggressive buying practices, poor relationships between retailers and producers, and disloyalty to national produce contributed to the Soil Association's decision to withhold its Organic Supermarket of the Year Award in 2001.[41]

Mainstream farm commentators, says research by the IIED, echo this suspicion, most strikingly for products such as milk, apples and potatoes, with little post-farm processing.[42] Some comments include (note that the average cost of production for milk is 21p a litre):

> *The income generated at the farm gate is a fraction of that taken at the supermarket checkout. In our [2001] survey, dairy farmers achieved an average price of 18p a litre for milk. Even a large 4-pint container of milk costs nearly three times that [per litre].*
>
> Mark Hill, leader of Deloitte & Touche's Food & Agriculture team[43]

A large number of dairy farmers have felt the direct impact of the power of the supermarkets, as they are left with fewer and fewer alternative outlets for their produce. We are concerned that as primary producers, our margins are being squeezed to a point where most farmers are losing money, whilst the supermarkets appear to be able to maintain their margin at any price.

Director of large dairy farming business[44]

Supermarkets and their associated companies effectively have the farmers over a barrel. You either accept their prices or you don't trade. And that reflects in lower prices at markets.

Richard North, writer and meat analyst[45]

Retailers cannot deny the truth about profiteering on potatoes. With meat they can hide behind processing charges and differences in the value of various parts of carcasses. Potatoes are processed and delivered in retailers' own bags. All they have to do is display the product and collect a huge mark up at the tills.

Jane Howells, Farmers' Union of Wales[46]

Growers are leaving the industry, never to return, because there is so little margin in it. Growers need a price that doesn't just keep

*their heads above water, but allows them to
reinvest, for the future good of the industry.*

Graham Nichols, NFU Potato Committee
chairman[47]

**What you get is a telephone call on a
Thursday, saying 'We're going on
promotion next week, so the price is
going down by £30 a ton or £40 a ton or
£50 a ton and we're on promotion for
two weeks.' And you do the two weeks
and the following week you're still on the
same price even though the retail price
may go up.**

Richard Bingham, brassica grower in
Lincolnshire[48]

A survey of over 100 British apple and pear growers in
1999 showed that 85 per cent felt that the supermarkets were not giving them a fair deal.[49] The following
chart shows the average difference between farm-gate
and retail prices in the UK according to the National
Farmers' Union.

Average difference between farm-gate and retail prices [50]

Commodity	Measure value	Farm-gate value	Retailer receives	% farmer receives
Beef	£/kg	£1.72	£6.58	26%
Lamb	£/kg	£2.24	£4.57 (shoulder)	49%
Pork	£/kg	£0.95	£4.78 (loin)	20%
Chicken	£/kg	£0.49	£2.32 (fresh)	21%
Bacon	£/kg	£0.96	£6.97 (back)	14%
Milk	£/pint	£0.09	£0.36	25%
Eggs	£/dozen	£0.32	£1.51	21%
Apples, dessert	£/kg	£0.33	£1.26	26%
Potatoes	£/kg	£0.07	£0.91	8%
Tomatoes	£/kg	£0.56	£1.10	51%
Cauliflower	£/kg	£0.33	£0.81	41%
Carrots	£/kg	£0.16	£0.58	28%
Onions	£/kg	£0.17	£0.73	23%
Strawberries	£/kg	£2.21	£4.26	52%
Bread (wheat flour)	£/kg	£0.06	£0.74	8%
Total cost of basket		**£11.29**	**£37.48**	**26%**

Responding to accusations of profiteering from the foot-and-mouth disease and a predicted glut in British meat, the supermarkets insisted, according to the IIED, that they:

> *have told their large processors [that] they*
> *expect them to hold cost prices at pre-crisis*
> *levels as well as maintain prices paid to*
> *farmers.*[51]

But some UK farmers, angry at increased cheap imports, consider that workers in dedicated 'primary marketing organisations' (importers):

> *may as well be wearing the same uniforms*
> *as the supermarkets.*[52]

The UK government has been slow to recognise this and only focuses on retail prices reflecting the trends of the farm-gate price, not what products sell for at the till. Its Department for Environment, Food and Rural Affairs (DEFRA) concludes that in UK red-meat markets in the 1990s, the greater part of farm-gate price changes for beef, pork and lamb (70 to 90 per cent) were eventually passed down the supply chain to retail prices. However the process was not instantaneous, averaging about four months before farm-gate price changes were fully reflected in retail prices. For the 1990s as a whole, supermarkets were found to be slower to cut their prices in response to a fall in farm-gate prices than to put up prices when farm products became more expensive. The

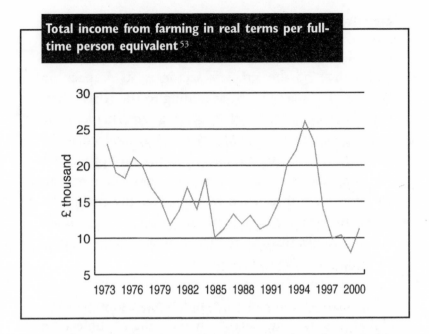

Total income from farming in real terms per full-time person equivalent [53]

government's final conclusions are that from 1998 onwards retail prices did become more responsive to changes in farm-gate prices.[54]

In 2000, according to DEFRA, the total income from farming in the UK was at its lowest level in real terms since the depression of the late 1930s, although there has been a small recovery (see above). For some farm households the downturn is being partly cushioned by other sources of income. More than a half of full-time farms in England have diversified sources of income (either through off-farm employment or other types of business on the farm, such as B&B or cheese production) and for a significant number this is at present more important than the income earned from farming.[55]

Impacts on farming

One of the most controversial elements of supermarket dominance of the grocery sector is its impact on farming. For many years, according to the IIED, there have been accusations that the big supermarkets are reaping excessive profits from the agri-food chain by turning the screw on suppliers and primary producers. Farmers in developing countries also complain that their livelihoods are threatened by unjust supply-chain relationships for their export production. This squeeze on farming is affecting the resilience of the rural economy and quality of the environment. [56]

Although the industry has been found to be broadly competitive, the sheer scale and buying power of the global supermarket giants makes them subject to increasing scrutiny, as well as discontent among farmers that has occasionally resulted in militant action against stores and depots. Around 233,000 UK farmers trade with the majority of the population via only a handful of supermarket companies, where UK consumers purchase 75–80 per cent of their groceries. The profit of all of those farms has been roughly equivalent to the profit of just six supermarket chains in the past two years, as the table below shows.[57]

The IIED warns that UK farming has seen a massive slump in income since 1995, and is now at its lowest point for 60 years. In 2001, the average 200-hectare UK farm made £2,500 from agriculture. Farmers are working a 70-hour week for the equivalent of working for 70p an hour (less than a quarter of the minimum wage). UK farming is contracting, demoralised and

Supermarkets versus farming profits[58]			
	Net Profit 1991 (£m)	Net Profit 2000(£m)	Net Profit 2001 (£m)
Combined top 6 supermarkets	2,030 (est.)	1,611 (est.)	1,712
UK agriculture (233,000 holdings)	2,358	1,540	1,710 (est.)

ageing. Mid-sized professional farmers are suffering the most, being tied to the land with no chance of taking off-farm work. The crisis is spread across all sectors; cereals, dairy, egg and poultry, livestock and horticulture. The knock-on effects are considerable; the NFU has spoken of growing problems affecting Britain's farming industry, which could force thousands to leave the land, with low incomes, job losses and poor prices leading to a new crisis in agriculture.[59]

Farmers who have attempted to diversify by converting to organic production have come up against a flood of imports, despite evidence of high retail margins for organic produce. Opportunities to bypass supermarkets by directly marketing at farmers' markets, which have grown exponentially since 1998 to over 300, are still tiny, however; the estimated total farmers' markets sales of £65 million still represent only around 0.12 per cent of total food expenditure in the UK. [60]

The supermarkets, in turn, point to high levels of concentration in the processing/packing industry and state that they have little control over the trading relationship between farmers and the processors. Of course, much of that concentration is driven by the supermarkets themselves, as they prefer to deal with a small number (forecast soon to be a only a handful) of fresh-produce suppliers to help achieve their quality assurance and 'traceability' (ie awareness of who produced a product) objectives.[61]

Charles Secret of Thames Valley Growers has claimed that:

> *Supermarkets have had a devastating impact on our industry . . . they have virtually decimated what were rich, varied production areas by taking their business abroad. Growers have been de-skilled and de-tooled. Fewer and fewer crops are grown in the UK, which was once self-sufficient in fruit and vegetables . . . As long as people continue to buy their fruit and vegetables in supermarkets, I really don't think UK growing has much of a future.*[62]

Code of practice

Following the Competition Commission's extensive inquiry into the industry in 2000, a 'Code of Practice on Supermarkets' Dealings with Suppliers' was recommended (although no sanctions were imposed).[63] Many farm groups welcomed the Code, details of which were then negotiated between the major supermarkets and the government's Office of Fair Trading (OFT) (see below).

Code of Practice on Supermarkets' Dealings with Suppliers [64]

Part 1: Standard terms of business

- Terms of business to be available in writing
- No undue delay in payments

Part 2: Prices & payments

- No retrospective reduction in price without reasonable notice

- No obligation to contribute to marketing costs:

    (a) buyer visits to new or prospective suppliers;

    (b) artwork or packaging design;

    (c) consumer or market research;

    (d) the opening or refurbishing of a store; or

    (e) hospitality for that supermarket's staff.

- No payments for lower profits unless the basis of payment is agreed in advance

- No payments for wastage without prior agreement, negligence or default

- Limited circumstances for lump-sum payments as a condition of being a supplier

- No lump sum payments for better positioning of goods unless in relation to promotions

Part 3: Promotions

- No promotions without reasonable notice

- Due care to be taken when ordering for promotions

- Suppliers not predominantly to fund promotions

Part 4: Compensation

- No change to supply chain procedures without reasonable notice or compensation

- No change to specifications without reasonable notice or compensation

- Limited circumstances for compensation for erroneous forecasts

Part 5: Consumer complaints

- No unjustified payment for consumer complaints

Part 6: Third party dealings

- No tying third-party goods and services for payment

Part 7: Staff training

- Obligatory training for buyers

Part 8: General

- Compliance and dispute resolution

- Interpretation

But the final Code from the Department of Trade and Industry (DTI), which came into effect on 17 March 2002 and which is (on the insistence of the Commission) applicable only to the top four supermarkets, was roundly criticised for the inclusion of 'weasel words' that allow wide interpretation by retailers. A 'Fair Deal Group' has been set up by a grouping of trade associations (including the Country Land and

Business Association, the British Print Industry Association and the British Packaging Federation) to 'help small suppliers make their complaints about unfair trade practices used by supermarkets anonymously.'[65]

Friends of the Earth, with the support of farming and public interest organisations, carried out a survey of farmers in February 2003 to find out how farmers were faring under the Code and in general under current market conditions.[66] Key findings included:[67]

- Less than half of the respondents (44 per cent) were aware that a Code of Practice had been introduced in March 2002, and most had not seen a copy.

- More than half of the farmers who responded (58 per cent) did not think that the OFT Code of Practice had made any difference to the way supermarkets did business with them.

- All four supermarkets currently bound by the Code of Practice (Tesco, Asda, Sainsbury's and Safeway) were named by farmers in connection with practices being of concern by the Competition Commission.

- A significant proportion of farmers who responded (eg 5 per cent of dairy farmers) said they were getting paid the same as or less than the price of production for their produce.

- There was strong support from respondents for new legislation to prohibit the unfair trading practices of the supermarkets, and for an independent regulator to oversee the way supermarkets do business with their suppliers. Respondents also supported the proposal that supermarkets should be required to source a proportion of food locally.

- About a third of respondents who had experienced problems supplying supermarkets said that 'fear of delisting' was their reason for not complaining.

Friends of the Earth claim that the OFT Code of Practice is simply not working. Supermarket behaviour is not changing, unfair trading continues to be the norm and this situation is unlikely to change unless action is taken. A strong regulatory approach is needed to bring the power of the supermarkets under control, protect small independent shops and get a fair deal for farmers for their produce. At the same time, there is a need for greater support for alternative and innovative ways of selling groceries, such as local food schemes, where food is sold locally to where it is produced.[68]

Ban on whistle blowing

As mentioned earlier, growers do not feel they could complain about supermarkets, as this could can lead to being dropped as a supplier or delisted. One respondent to Friends of the Earth's survey said they'd love to give their contact details:

> *but if leaked to supermarkets I would be delisted and so forced out of business.*[69]

Another supplier giving evidence to the Competition Commission said:

> *It would be commercial suicide for any supplier to give a true and honest account of all aspects of relationships with retailers.*[70]

John Breach, chairman of the British Independent Fruit Growers Association confirmed that:

> *Suppliers fear that if they revert to the Code of Practice they might be delisted by the supermarkets.*[71]

The Competition Commission referred to the 'climate of apprehension' among suppliers. This has had a devastating impact on UK farmers and growers;[72] a consultant to the packaging industry noted to the Commission that:

> *The degree and variety of pressure upon the suppliers was extremely alarming; all complied with the retailers' demands because of the dread of delisting.*[73]

Safeway merger

Since the Competition Commission's conclusions on the supermarket industry in 2000, has the industry addressed its impacts on suppliers and farmers? Its report on the Safeway takeover in 2003 found that suppliers had the following concerns about the big supermarkets:[74]

> *The supermarkets use their buying power to force suppliers to reduce their prices or otherwise accept lower returns, for instance by compelling them to bear costs that should properly be regarded as the retailer's or to give discounts on supplies.*

> *Further concentration in the supermarket industry is bound to exacerbate suppliers' problems. There was a fear that, if Safeway was acquired by any of the bidders (Tesco, Sainsbury's, Asda and Morrisons), the efforts of weaker supermarkets to retain market share through even harsher terms for suppliers will do further damage to suppliers.*

> *Intense buying power and internationalisation of procurement will damage UK farming and primary production.*

> *Trading conditions make it impossible for suppliers to raise prices to the large*

supermarkets (some took the same view of prices to smaller retailers as well).

Many suppliers, faced with large supermarkets' buying power, saw their only option was to cut costs, especially those of research and product innovation, leading eventually to reduced consumer choice.

The OFT Code of Practice has failed to curb what several of the submissions referred to as predatory practices.

Asda's acquisition by Wal-Mart marked a fundamental change in multiple food retailing in the UK. In response, its competitors (most notably Tesco) had intensified the price and cost pressures they exerted on both large and small suppliers.

The supermarkets' response to these accusations were as follows:[75]

(a) Asda said that it had traditionally had good relationships with suppliers. In 2002, it had commissioned research concluded that suppliers were generally positive in their attitudes to Asda. It said that it co-operated with its suppliers, in particular giving them access to its Retail Link information system, allowing them to retrieve sales data regarding their products.

Asda considered that its good supplier relations meant that the Code had limited impact on it. But it recognised that the Code might protect small suppliers in the event of a strengthening of Asda's bargaining position if it acquired Safeway. In the case of large suppliers, the impact of the Code, (which made no distinction between suppliers on the basis of size), would remain minimal. These suppliers, particularly large multinational and national food and beverage manufacturers, were in a position to look after their own interests without recourse to the Code. Asda said that it viewed its 'everyday low prices' policy as allowing products to compete solely on the attraction of the value and choice they provide, avoiding the distortion of competition from promotions. While some procurement of its non-grocery products was undertaken internationally or globally by Wal-Mart, all procurement of grocery products (including non-food items such as toiletries and household cleaners traditionally sold by multiple grocery retailers) was undertaken by Asda itself, except bananas (because of the relative uniformity of the product and the small number of suppliers worldwide, which made international buying sensible).

(b) Morrisons said that it had strong positive relationships with suppliers, whose critical part in the supply chain to consumers it recognised. Its policy was to keep its buyers responsible for the same product areas for as long as possible. Its vertically integrated approach meant that it dealt directly with many primary producers and its emphasis on fresh food meant that 55 per cent of sales were own-label products bought from a broad supply base including many small suppliers. Nevertheless, its relations with large branded suppliers remained as good as, if not better than, at the time of the 2000 report. However, Morrisons considered the manufacturers of leading brands to be powerful, arguing that consolidation of the UK supply base had taken place since 2000. It reminded us that it was not a signatory to the Code, although DEFRA had suggested that it might wish to become one. However, it believed that, as it had excellent relationships with its suppliers and its purchasing procedures exceeded the requirements of the Code, there would be no benefit to its suppliers if it became a signatory.

(c) Sainsbury's said that it had historically had good relations with its suppliers, who particularly valued its use of promotions and new-product development. It had effective machinery for the resolution of disputes with suppliers and considered that the Code had worked well. It had an existing Code of its own that was updated to ensure consistency with the OFT Code.

(d) Tesco stressed that its relationships with its suppliers were based upon maintaining a mutually advantageous trading relationship. While the manufacturers of leading brands supplied all multiple grocery retailers, retailers' choices of smaller suppliers were an important factor in their ability to differentiate their offerings to consumers. Tesco did not consider that the OFT Code had significantly altered its relationships with its suppliers. It acknowledged that its buying terms tended to be better than those obtained by smaller multiple grocery retailers, but believed that any differences in buyer power among the main parties were much less significant. Any differences in the cost prices achieved by the large national multiple grocery retailers reflected differences in technical efficiency and skill in buying rather than in intrinsic buyer power.

The International Institute for Environment and Development concluded that the process of consolidation in retail still has a long way to go. Wal-Mart has grown to become not only the world's biggest retailer, but also the biggest grocer, with US grocery sales estimated at $57 billion. Carrefour, Ahold and Wal-Mart have become truly global in their reach; in 2000, these three companies alone had sales (food and non-food) of $300 billion, profits of $8 billion and employed 1.9 million people. It is predicted that there will be only 10 major global food retailers by 2010. A similar trend is taking place in food processing and distribution, in order to prevent market power and profits slipping down the food chain.[76]

The verdict

The actions against suppliers and farmers by supermarkets go way beyond efficient business practices. It is incredible that the OFT Code of Practice has not become a legal document, bearing in mind that the contents of the code are minimum standards of practice only. It is clear that supermarkets' policies are affecting the viability of individual companies as well as the whole farming industry. The enormous buying power of the top four or five supermarkets means that suppliers and farmers have little alternative but to put up with the arsenal of price-cutting practices the supermarkets throw at them. Essentially, the supermarkets have transferred all the risk of making a loss or becoming bankrupt onto suppliers and farmers. This risk is now a way of life for these suppliers and farmers, who live in fear of complaining or fighting back.

Chapter 3

Communities

The benefits of having a locally run and locally owned store is really about providing the best form of adaptability to customer needs and the best focal point for the local community in the shop. They're [supermarkets] effectively a monopoly and therefore should be treated as such. We are not asking for protection from this government to make major interventions and check supermarket power to the extreme. What we are looking for is some simple regulatory changes that will protect consumers and retailers and suppliers from the worse excesses of supermarket behaviour. It's a conscious choice: the choice is do you want the market to prevail and therefore accept the potentially reduction in choice and independence, variety and independence in the grocery market, particularly in the smaller end, or do government want to take action that will preserve that choice and more sustainable retail market in the long run?

Shane Brennan, Spokesperson,
Association of Convenience Stores, 23/01/04

Consumers can see first-hand the effect of supermarkets on communities, although they, along with supermarkets and policy makers, do not seem to recognise this connection. The most obvious example is out-of-town supermarkets draining trade away from town and village centres, leaving them with fast-food outlets, discount stores and fewer independent retailers. With the added pressure of fierce competition, independent local shops such as greengrocers, bakers and butchers and now banks and chemists are disappearing from our high streets and communities. This leads not only to the loss of local shops but also a dearth of choice of products and real competition. Another consequence is unemployment; supermarkets cannot match this loss with new jobs, as they employ fewer staff and use national rather than local business services. Finally 'food deserts' – where people are unable to access locally the healthy and cheap food that most of us take for granted – have a dramatic effect, impacting most on the poor, elderly, disabled and people in remote communities.

Planning laws

Planning laws were tightened up in 1996 to slow down the out-of-town expansion of supermarkets. England, Scotland and Wales have slightly different regulations. The planning system in England is not designed to promote competition between retailers; the government has introduced a 'scale of need' system to assess the degree to which a local community needs a new supermarket. However, these regulations are unclear and open to interpretation.

In Wales, the situation is a little better; if a new out-of-centre supermarket is 'likely to lead to the loss of general food retailing in the centre of small towns', then this is grounds for a refusal. In Scotland, a supermarket planning application cannot be refused because the local community does not need a new supermarket.[1]

Independent retailers

The New Economics Foundation (a social think tank) researched the decline of communities, producing a report called 'Ghost Town Britain'. It explains how we used to be a nation of shopkeepers, but have become a nation of shop-busters. Local shops and services, including corner shops, grocers, high-street banks, post offices, pubs and hardware stores are fast disappearing. The change is happening most visibly in villages and market towns, but just as dramatically in many larger urban and suburban areas. Between 1995 and 2000 we lost roughly one-fifth of these vital institutions; the very fabric of our local economies. If current trends continue, we will lose one-third of the tattered remains over the next ten years. The result is Ghost Town Britain, where an increasing number of communities and neighbourhoods will lack easy access to local banks, post offices, corner shops and pubs that provide the social glue holding communities together.[2]

If you combine the decline in the number of banks, post offices, pubs, food retailers and general non-specialised stores (usually corner shops), what emerges is a cumulative loss of over 30,000 local economic outlets across the country in the five years up to the year 2000 alone, with a further 28,000 forecast to be lost by 2005. The number of local shops is expected to have fallen by nearly one-third between 1990 and 2010, with many smaller communities in the UK no longer having any such institutions by 2010. In a few, low-income neighbourhoods the death-knell for essential elements of the local economy has already sounded; over the next ten years it will become commonplace.[3]

Supermarkets seem to have effectively identified and satisfied consumer preferences, as their huge success among the UK population – and market share – suggests. However, supermarkets have also brought negative impacts; the food charity Sustain itemises concentration in the food sector (particularly in fresh produce); a major decline in specialist, independent stores (butchers, bakers, greengrocers, etc); and a decline in the availability of regional produce. With their large purchasing and marketing power, supermarkets have out-competed smaller independent stores; from 1980 to 1994 the percentage of food sold by independent retailers fell from 31 per cent to 22 per cent and the number of independent retailers declined by 25 per cent.[4]

Losing such local facilities can lead to food and enterprise deserts, loss of employment, loss of outlets for local products and services, reduction of diversity of cultural and retail environments, and environmental impacts due to car-based shopping (ie out-of-town supermarkets usually require consumers to drive rather than walk). The arrival of a supermarket has a huge impact on the viability of a rural community, resulting in village shops within a seven-mile radius inevitably closing down. Friends of the Earth states that money spent in supermarkets does not remain in the community the way that money spent in local businesses does.[2] In a survey the charity carried out in Ludlow, more than 80 per cent of local food shops sold some local produce, and for many it was a large proportion of their sales, whereas supermarkets tend to import food into the region.[5]

Colin Breed MP warns that Wal-Mart's acquisition of Asda in 1999 marked the beginning of a new retail chapter, with supermarkets now following the US group's practice of offering a wider range of products, such as electrical goods and clothing. This diversification means that a new supermarket in an area now leaves few sectors of the local retail infrastructure untouched by its presence. Certainly, the recent expansion of the supermarkets' brands into the service industries of banking, pharmacies, photo-developing and even divorce services (to mention just a few) signals that little has been done to protect the heterogeneity necessary for healthy consumer relations. Consumer choice is rapidly becoming little more than a decision about which supermarket to choose, with over 95 per cent of people in the UK doing their main shopping at a supermarket.[6]

The benefits gained from preserving our smaller independent food stores are significant. It is argued by Sustain that these include:[7]

- **Promotion of local diversity and food culture.**

- **Fresher produce.**

- **Boosting the local economy by supporting local businesses and therefore jobs, and indirectly other businesses (the 'multiplier effect').**

In a move that drove another nail into the coffin of independent traders, supermarket giant Tesco took another leap towards dominance of Britain's food shopping in 2002 by buying the country's second biggest chain of corner shops, T&S Stores. Tesco, which already has the principal 18 per cent share of the supermarket trade, paid £377m for 850 convenience store outlets, mainly in the Midlands but also in the South and in the Northwest. More than half are to be converted into its Tesco Express format, which had previously been restricted to petrol stations. The move, which analysts say would restrict choice for the consumer by putting pressure on independent retailers, nevertheless extends a trend by the big supermarkets to invest in what is called the 'C-store sector'. After years of developing out-of-town superstore sites, which have now either reached saturation point or come up against opposition on environmental or planning grounds, supermarkets are muscling their way back into the high street.[8]

But there is talk of a local retail renaissance. The government has made a commitment to improving shopping access for poorer people, with action teams and taskforces aplenty. Most of the high-street banks have declared a halt on bank branch closures, while the Post Office said it would not close rural branches for the next five years. Meanwhile, farmers' markets, organic fruit and vegetable 'box schemes' (where households get deliveries of fresh produce to their door) and car-boot sales are evidence of a groundswell of popular resistance to the standardisation of how we shop.[9]

Unfortunately, according to the New Economics Foundation, all of these worthy initiatives and pilot projects are failing to counteract the far greater economic forces that are driving Ghost Town Britain. Despite the government's rhetoric in favour of sustaining small businesses and well-meaning work by community activists, action teams and taskforces, there is no let-up in the destruction of the local economy. As yet, there is no willingness to tackle the real reasons why Britain's towns are dying on their feet. These include increasing market domination by and preferential policy treatment of supermarkets; the failure to enforce the end of downsizing in banks and post offices; transport systems that encourage car travel; weak planning controls on out-of-town stores; and a lack of support for truly local enterprise. There is even alarming evidence that the UK retail market could be at 'tipping point', where the number of local shops could crash dramatically, rather than following the steady trend of decline.[10]

Why? It's a question of brutal economics. According to the New Economics Foundation, when the number of local retail outlets falls below a critical mass, the quantity of money circulating within the local economy will plummet sharply as people find there is no point trying to do a full shop with an impoverished range of local outlets. This is particularly true if people can no longer withdraw cash because of bank-branch or cash-point closure. The likelihood of hostile 'corporate actions' (mergers or acquisitions) means that the best intentions of organisations that manage large branch networks could be undone by newcomers with no commitment to local economies. Nor is the supermarkets' highly successful new C-store format the salvation of the local retail fabric. In fact, it is likely to undermine it still further by competing with independent shops in the same location, while providing all services under one compact, identikit roof but with no link between supplies and the local economy.[11]

Communities

But does it really matter? After all, modern consumers are well informed and if they choose to patronise the big multiple retailers, why should anyone object? The problem is that consumers themselves lament the loss of local shops, yet are caught in a vicious circle where choice and price, work and travel patterns, brands and advertising, all conspire to undermine the desire for a vibrant local economy. No individual consumer feels they can reverse this trend, despite feeling a sense of loss as long-established local institutions disappear one by one. The emergence of Ghost Town Britain is contributing to much more than a sense of powerlessness and nostalgia; it is creating a nation where:[12]

- Neighbourhoods become food and enterprise deserts with poor nutrition and ill health (eg diabetes, heart disease and mental health problems).

- People lose financial literacy because they no longer trade on a daily basis in the community.

- The poor fall prey to unscrupulous money-lending practices and overpriced, low-quality consumer goods.

- The unemployed lose informal routes back into work as part-time jobs disappear from the locality.

- Local entrepreneurs lose valuable local outlets for their products and services.

- Communities suffer a rapid loss of 'social capital' (ie neighbourliness, trust and shared values, social networks etc) and become victim to vandalism and more serious crime.

- The cultural and retail environment loses diversity and becomes impoverished.

- The environment and people's health suffer as people are forced into car-based shopping even for relatively short journeys.

Sustain states that supermarkets should contribute to rather than detract from the local community through redefining the role of the store as one that assists wealth to circulate and multiply within communities and regions. Supermarkets' sourcing strategies can have significant impacts on the local economy and the viability of suppliers, particularly small-scale producers and growers. The UK farming sector is now characterised by larger, fewer enterprises, whose 'efficiencies of scale' (ie intensive farming methods) mean fewer jobs for local people and the consequent impoverishment of the rural economy. According to Sustain, supermarkets have encouraged this trend, favouring the convenience of dealing with large-scale producers and dealers over a greater number of smaller suppliers. Regionally specific crop varieties and foods are also declining and, importantly, there is a greater risk of supply breakdown.[13]

As supermarkets have gained market share from independent and specialist stores, the wider local economy has been affected. Whereas a local store would probably use a local printing shop or firm of solicitors, a major multiple is likely to use national services contracted centrally. Food retailing employs 4 per cent of the national workforce. In 2001, 72,700 new jobs were created by the retail industry, 68 per cent of the new jobs across the economy as a whole. Yet one study by Sustain suggests that less than 16 per cent of supermarket turnover translates into local wages, purchases and services. The same study found that every £10 spent with a local food initiative is worth £25 to the local economy, compared with just £14 when the same amount is spent in a multiple supermarket, as its value increases in the local community by being reinvested many times over (often referred to as the 'multiplier effect').[14]

The New Economics Foundation also claims that supermarkets do not contribute to local economies in the same way as local shops. Very little of the wealth that supermarkets generate actually stays in the communities in which they operate. For example, Tesco's payroll makes up just seven per cent of its total turnover. The great bulk of the company's retail profits flow from the stores back to the head office, and ultimately to the corporation's shareholders around the world. Meanwhile, the construction of out-of-town superstores creates a vacuum that sucks resources from the town centres, strangling the heart of the local economy.[15]

There is now strong evidence that new food superstores have a negative net effect on retail employment. The New Economics Foundation estimates that a community can expect to lose about 276 jobs when a supermarket moves into its area, mostly from the small locally owned food shops, even taking into account the jobs newly available at the supermarket. Research on market towns and district centres shows that following the development of large edge or out-of-town superstores, local speciality shops and convenience stores lose anywhere from 21 to 75 per cent of their market share, forcing many to lay-off staff or close down entirely.[16]

UK government research published in 1988, for example, showed that edge-of-town and out-of-town supermarkets have a serious impact on between 13 and

50 per cent of the local market in market towns and centres.[17] Between 1991 and 1997 villages and market towns lost half of their small shops.[18] Another government report noted that the opening of one Tesco supermarket on the edge of the small market town of Cirencester, Wiltshire led to the market share of town-centre food shops declining by 38 per cent.[19] The Cornwall Association of Village Shopkeepers found that 202 jobs out of 270 were at risk from a supermarket,[20] and Campaign for the Protection of Rural England (CPRE) reported on the detrimental impact of an out-of-town superstore on farmers, local stores and employment in Suffolk, where a complex local network of supply and demand, along with jobs, shops and wholesalers, would be destroyed by the new store.[21] The Institute for Public Policy Research, one of Britain's leading think tanks, has calculated that a typical out-of-town supermarket has a subsidy of £25,000 per week over its town centre equivalent because the cost of the extra pollution and congestion from cars and delivery vehicles generated by the out-of-town store is borne by tax payers and the local community.[22]

Yet, deliberate action by supermarkets, taking into account local needs and conditions, and placing more custom with local businesses – both suppliers and service providers – could have a strong and positive effect on local economies. A change for the better will require greater emphasis on regional rather than national distribution patterns, and on redefining the role of the store as one that assists wealth to circulate and multiply within communities and regions.[23]

Food poverty

In a report for the International Institute for Environment and Development, Lindy Sharpe, a food poverty expert for Sustain, states that even amid abundance, the problems of hunger and insufficient food have not disappeared. 'Food poverty' is the inability to secure an adequate, nutritious diet because of lack of money, or an inability to get to shops that sell nutritious foods at affordable prices, or lack of cooking facilities or skill. A number of studies have confirmed that, although food choice is down to the individual, the range of choice is often limited by factors beyond the individual's control. In other words, if people do not eat well, this is not simply a matter of poor judgement or lack of information.[24]

The think tank Demos states that the food-retailing system caters better for the 'time poor, cash rich' than for the 'time poor, cash poor'; the transport system is better for car owners than those dependent on buses. When food retailing left the high street the poorest found themselves without adequate local food shops. Now that some shops have returned, they are set up to cater for a very different segment of society, such as the more affluent. Time and the food economy have moved on, but the poorest in British society remain disadvantaged.[25]

The associated rise in car-borne shopping has left car-less shoppers at a disadvantage, living in what Lindy Sharpe refers to as 'food deserts', with less access to cheaper, fresh food. Recent research in Sandwell in the West Midlands has found large networks of streets and estates where there are no shops selling fruit and/or vegetables; in these districts inexpensive, good-quality food is only available in concentrated shopping areas, which the majority of the population would have to travel to by car or public transport.[26]

However, it is misleading to ghettoise food poverty to sink estates or remote rural areas with no transport (although these areas undoubtedly suffer disproportionately). Sharpe reveals that many of the people who struggle to feed themselves satisfactorily include the elderly and the disabled (who might have mobility problems, difficulty carrying shopping or no access to a car); students, who are likely to be short of cash for fares and food, and often have inadequate cooking facilities; and immigrant groups. Take just one of these groups, the elderly, who now comprises one-sixth of the population. In 2001, 1 in 7 people over the age of 65 was malnourished or at serious risk of malnutrition. As a result, the elderly are more likely to be hospitalised, more likely to need extended hospital treatment and more likely to be re-admitted after discharge; a large and preventable cost to the National Health Service.[27] Sharpe lists the differentiating effects of poor nutrition as follows:[28]

- **Poor households eat less varied foods.**

- **People in poorer households are less likely to eat fresh fruit, wholemeal bread, lean meat and oily fish, all recommended for healthy living.**

- At all ages, people in poorer households have lower nutrient intakes than people in richer households, and the gap has widened over the past 20 years (see below).

- Pregnant women on low incomes have very poor diets and are more likely to bear low birthweight babies (who are likely to suffer health problems in later life).

- Children who are poorly nourished are unlikely to grow well; they are also more likely to become obese.

- Children who come to school hungry, with no breakfast, are less likely to benefit from schooling and learn well.

Poorer people tend to eat poor-quality food (ie high in fat and sugar) because it is cheaper and is usually more filling. Poor families spend a higher proportion of their smaller income on food – 27 per cent compared with 18 per cent for the rest of the population – but this, because of the smaller budget, still amounts to less pounds per household in real terms. Studies show that people in low-income households know which foods are healthy, but may be unable to buy them because they are unavailable, too expensive, or (in the case of perishable foods, such as fruit) they fear wastage. Research has also found that the cheapest calories come from the least nourishing foods (such as white bread and biscuits),

Comparison of consumption of food types for low compared to high-income families[29]

Food	Low income consumption compared to high income
Whole fat milk	+52%
Reduced fat milk	-13%
Sugar	+149%
Fresh green vegetables	-35%
Fresh fruit	-48%
White bread	+129%
Wholemeal bread	-27%
Fresh fish	-64%
Frozen fish products	+34%
Polyunsaturated oils	-10%
Fibre	-19%
Calcium	-6%
Iron	-15%
Vitamin A	-22%
Vitamin C	-38%

and that more nutritious foods have increased in price more steeply than less nutritious equivalents. For example, between 1984 and 1998, wholemeal bread rose in price by 30 per cent and fresh potatoes by 120 per cent, whereas white, sliced bread rose only by 18 per cent and frozen chips by 26 per cent. And 100 calories derived from custard cream biscuits cost 2.4p, while 100 calories from fresh pork chops cost 26.5p, from cabbage 30p, from full fat milk 6.2p and from skimmed milk 12.1p.[30]

The NHS Plan, a long-term investment strategy for the National Health Service, acknowledges that while people make their own choices about what to eat, it is the government's job to ensure people have 'proper access to healthy food wherever they live'. It can work; the Fat Watch campaign in the Netherlands shows how a partnership between supermarkets and other private-sector partners reduced the consumption of saturated fats over a five-year period from 16.4 per cent to 14.1 per cent of energy intake. Elements of this campaign were, for example, supermarket tours guided by a dietician and brochures. One supermarket chain sponsored a magazine in which they regularly pay attention to topics about healthy nutrition.[31]

Of course, supermarkets are not responsible for the nation's diet and cannot single-handedly change it for the better, even if philosophical questions about the role of the nanny state versus individual responsibility could be easily resolved. Retailers do not determine what people put into their trolleys, and they do not control the increasing portion of our diets that comes from caterers (eg restaurants, fast-food outlets, etc). But if individual shoppers choose what to buy, retailers – ie supermarkets – determine the range of choice available; what lines to stock, the prices and where to locate stores.[32]

Lindy Sharpe's report ultimately found that supermarkets' market power gives them a unique opportunity to initiate and support proposals that could actually improve the balance of diet and reduce health inequalities, two central goals of public-health policy. Supermarkets could develop policies in the following areas:[33]

- Siting new stores or refurbishing existing ones.

- Pricing, to ensure foods supportive of health do not cost more than less nutritious alternatives and do not cost more in deprived areas.

- Improving access to stores other than by car.

- Which foods to sell and how much display space to allocate to them, to support rather than undermine advice on healthy eating.

The verdict

There is ample evidence that supermarkets have contributed to the decline of local communities in terms of loss of local retailers and jobs, as well as the creation of food deserts. Consumers are often denied an alternative to supermarkets because there simply are no independent retailers. People without cars have suffered the most by not having access to local amenities in terms of jobs and trade as well as cheap, healthy food.

The supermarkets have come up with some initiatives – such as Tesco with its regeneration programme, see below – to appease critics, but these are relatively few and far between and still do not address the roots of the problem, which is supermarkets taking trade away from communities. Essentially, consumers and government need to recognise the links between the expansion of the supermarket industry and problems in local communities. Action needs to be taken to pressurise supermarkets to address these problems and to support local communities through consumer demand and government policy.

Tesco's regeneration programme [34]

Our regeneration schemes aim to bring together public services, employers and community groups to yield social, economic and environmental change in deprived urban areas. They are based around the development of a new store to serve the local community. By investing in these areas, we hope to attract other companies to invest there too, thus bringing improvements in economic prosperity.

Below are some examples of the stores that have already opened, creating opportunities and employment in local communities:

Seacroft, Leeds

Seacroft was Tesco's first regeneration partnership culminating in the opening of the store in November 2000. Seacroft was once one of the largest council estates in Europe and, despite sell-offs and stock transfer, 53 per cent of the population still live in council-owned accommodation. The resident population of Seacroft in mid-1998 was 18,200 people, but there were only 3,900 jobs in the area. In August 1998 there were 2,290 Income Support claimants in Seacroft; 17 per cent of its adult population, compared to 9 per cent for Leeds as a whole, and an average of 8 per cent for the UK overall. Out of the 8,414 English wards, Seacroft was ranked the 388th most deprived.

The Seacroft partnership involved a wide range of partners; Leeds City Council, the Employment Service, East Leeds Family Learning Centre and a group of local employers led by Tesco. The resulting partnership involved training for up to a year with guaranteed jobs at the end. The Tesco Extra store opened in November 2000, employing over 240 previously unemployed local people, many of whom had been out of work for more than two years.

Dragonville, Durham

Dragonville is a former mining and industrial area situated on the edge of Durham. The area is one of high social housing and is ranked 332nd most deprived area in the country. The resident population of the Dragonville area in mid-1998 was 2,200 but there were only 600 jobs in the area and 16 per cent of its adult population was on Income Support.

The Tesco Extra store opened in November 2001, creating 340 new jobs, 296 of which went to locally unemployed people.

Beckton, London

Beckton is one of the most deprived areas in London. Blighted by job loss in manufacturing and its docks, the area also has a very high number of residents for whom English is not their first language. The resident population of Beckton in mid-1998 was 6,300, but there were only 400 jobs. In August 1998 there were 1,105 Income Support claimants in Beckton and it was considered to be the 79th most deprived local authority ward in England.

The 109,000 square feet Tesco Extra opened in September 2002, creating 400 jobs.

Alloa, Scotland

Employment in the market town of Alloa was traditionally based on the manufacture of textiles, brewing and glass making. The decline of these industries left the town with relatively high unemployment and a deteriorating town centre. The Tesco Regeneration store, located on the site of an old yarn mill, created over 100 jobs specifically targeted at the local long-term unemployed.

Chapter 4

The Environment

*I really struggled on environment. You picked
up such a massive role, from ethics to transport,
through contaminated land to recycling and
waste; it's a huge, huge task. The PR machine
works ahead of the whole organisation and
that is definitely the case for environment. They
saw environment as a way of getting wacky
stories in the press. As Environmental Manager,
I was treated with ridicule and suspicion
within the organisation. They called you
swampy. They do do good environmental work,
but only if it pays back in under two years. But
shifting production to Vietnam and Cambodia
and pulling in organics from Hungary and
Poland, where the conditions are not nearly as
well monitored to my mind. Sainsbury's are
most serious about what they are doing about
environment. I think Waitrose and M&S are
serious about what they are doing about
environment. Tesco is less so. Morrisons are
honestly not doing it, they honestly do what the
have to with the bare minimum because they*

*are 'no frills'. And I think Asda are the ones
who really big up what they are doing with
nothing behind them.*

Ex Supermarket Environmental Manager,
February 2004

At first glance supermarkets do not necessarily seem to
have a significant environmental impact. Compared to
a power station or a chemical factory perhaps, supermarkets look 'clean', with only the supermarket building
being the obvious environmental problem (in terms of
electricity usage). In fact supermarkets, because of the
combination of selling consumer products and controlling enormous supply chains, have an enormous negative impact on the environment.

The first issue is the waste that supermarkets produce;
from transport packaging to superficially 'flawed' (but
still edible) fruit and vegetables. This chapter also looks
at the huge influence supermarkets have on the agricultural industry, and how this is responsible for the loss
of wildlife in the UK and abroad. Another major area
of concern is the excessive use of pesticides on the food
we eat. And supermarkets contribute significantly to
global warming, one of the greatest threats to the environment, through 'food miles' – ie flying much of our
food across the world so that we can have strawberries
and mange tout around the year. Another thorny environmental issue for supermarkets and consumers is
animal welfare; the cruel conditions that animals are
often bred and slaughtered in for our food enjoyment,
and the devastation of fish stocks around the world.

Packaging and waste

The UK produces over 78 million tonnes of commercial and industrial waste each year. According to Rupert Howes at the think tank Forum for the Future, perhaps 60 per cent of this waste ends up in the UK's diminishing number of landfill sites, while some 40 per cent is recycled.[1]

The UK food industry accounts for seven to eight million tonnes of waste sent to landfill – only topped by the ten million tonnes from the metals sector. This includes biodegradable and non-biodegradable waste; anything from production surpluses or trimmings to out-of-date tins.[2]

Supermarkets clearly have a role to play in reducing this total. The UK government's Department for the Environment, Food and Rural Affairs (DEFRA) estimates that supermarkets alone generate 200,000 tonnes of compostable material every year, but encouraging the environmentally friendly disposal of such material has proved difficult.[3] Food packaging also uses energy and creates pollution. Depressingly, Corporate Watch reports that 'supermarkets have persistently lobbied against returnable packaging as [it is] too labour intensive, refusing to stock it.' Of all the manufacturing industries, the food industry makes the largest demand on packaging, and finding ways to reduce this packaging quantity and its subsequent waste is a demanding task.[4]

Waste is another problem. According to Andy Jones in his report for Sustain and Elm Farm Research Centre, between 40 and 50 per cent of raw vegetables or salad may be rejected by large retailers at various stages along a production line, simply as a result of physical 'flaws'.[5] Suppliers may have to over-produce for supermarkets – particularly when running promotions – to cope with spikes in demand, which results in wastage. On top of that, there are end-of-promotion stock, production trials, underweight packs, products that flop, wrongly packaging goods and products past best-before dates,[6] all of which produce waste. Some of these substandard food products may be sold for use in prisons or hospitals but, in general, market barriers restrict the use of such products for other applications.[7]

On the plus side, waste minimisation initiatives are slowly being introduced. The Co-operative Group and Sainsbury's donate food surpluses to homeless people. FareShare (a charity helping the homeless) distributes 1,500 tonnes a year supplied by retailers and manufacturers to homeless charities and plans to double the volumes it redistributes nationwide over the next three years.[8] Safeway donates 370 tonnes of fresh food waste a year to local charities and Marks and Spencer recovers IT equipment for re-use and uses recycled materials in packaging.[9] Colin Breed MP from the Liberal Democrats states that recently packaging companies such as packaging technology.com have been looking into biodegradable packaging, including fruit trays, cling film and plastic nets all made from starch, which can be disposed of in the garden and acts as a fertiliser. Tesco now packages its organic fruit range this way and, if the project is successful, this could be a significant step towards bringing packaging waste levels under control.[10]

Furthermore, there has been talk of introducing a 9p tax on plastic bags that would be passed on to the consumer, forcing them to rethink their attitude to supermarket carrier bags. Supermarkets have been broadly supportive of this idea, which has already been a success in the Republic of Ireland. This would accelerate the uptake of current re-usable bag schemes run by UK supermarkets such as Sainsbury's and Waitrose, and could greatly reduce the 10 billion bags a year that we use in Britain.[11]

Nature conservation

One of the most crucial aspects of the environment is the diversity of life on our planet. 'Biodiversity' refers to the variability among living organisms and species and the ecological complexes they are part of; it therefore embraces the variety of all life on earth. Food retailers have direct impact on biodiversity and landscapes, for example from the construction of new stores and from the effects of transport. They also have significant influence over the more indirect impacts of activities within their supply chain.[12]

Food-production practices can have a major impact, both positive and negative, on biodiversity, from domesticated crops and livestock grown all over world, to products sourced from the wild, such as fish. Hannah Bartram from the Royal Society for the Protection of Birds (RSPB) suggests that the intensification of agriculture has damaged biodiversity, and there have been several instances of species becoming extinct (such as the Corn Bunting formally found in Northern Ireland) alongside the general rapid decline in farmland birds in Europe over the last two decades.[13]

Furthermore, farming methods of specialisation and intensification have resulted in agricultural landscapes with a 'low degree of variability' (ie we no longer have the richly varied landscapes, flora and fauna of old). This, combined with the use of artificial fertilisers and pesticides, plus changes in groundwater tables, cropping patterns and stocking densities, has led to large-scale losses or degradation of domestic and wild species and agro-ecosystems. These, ironically, often include species that support agriculture through pollination or natural pest control, such as bees, butterflies, hoverflies, lacewings and ladybirds.[14] Small, less intensive farms, on the other hand, have been shown to be less polluting, better for employment, better for wildlife and environmental diversity than large farms and, happily for them, more productive per acre.[15]

The RSPB states that supermarkets are not entirely responsible for encouraging farmers to protect and maintain the countryside's biodiversity, landscapes and historic heritage; there is a clear role for public policy and appropriate agri-environment schemes. However, supermarkets can play a significant role in supporting farmers who supply their produce to adopt more biodiversity and landscape friendly practices, by integrating additional requirements into their existing 'farm-assurance schemes'. These are organisations, such as

Assured British Pigs, The Freedom Food scheme, Organic Certification and the Real Meat Company, that farmers can join to show they comply with certain welfare standards. Of course the more complex the supply chain (perhaps involving primary marketing organisations), the more difficult it is for supermarkets to encourage suppliers to implement environment plans on their farms.[16]

Supermarkets should at least develop with their suppliers a strategy and timetable for ensuring that all primary produce sold is sourced from farms that are complying with environmental standards, and in particular a requirement for a whole farm environment audit and/or plan.[17] However, the RSPB states that simply adding extra conditions of supply to already demanding production specifications is not the whole answer. Companies in the food system must recognise the need to reward and share the costs of higher standards. In many cases, this might involve lobbying governments to provide incentives. Sometimes, it may be a question of informing consumers about the impacts of different production practices so that they can make a reasoned choice in favour of sustainable food products, and pay premiums where necessary. Finally, retailers and other stakeholders, including their critics – such as environmental and food pressure groups Friends of the Earth and Sustain – must be prepared to have a rational and realistic debate about how standards can be raised in an equitable and long-lasting manner.[18]

Pesticides

Supermarkets tend to choose varieties of fruit and vegetables based on strict requirements on their shelf lives and appearance. To comply with this, farmers use more pesticides: a survey by Friends of the Earth of apple growers in 2003 found more than half of respondents admitting that they had to apply more pesticides to meet the cosmetic standards of the supermarkets. Excessive use of pesticides can lead to pesticide residues in our food, which could cause health issues particularly for children, and water pollution affecting drinking-water supplies.[19]

Government tests for pesticide residues show that 46 per cent of apples sold in supermarkets in 1998–2001 contained pesticide residues, with 18 per cent containing more than one pesticide. If supermarkets opted for varieties more resistant to disease (but less uniform in appearance and with a shorter shelf life) this could cut the amount of pesticides applied to our food. Although some smaller supermarkets such as Co-op, Waitrose and Marks and Spencer have made a commitment to reducing pesticides in their produce, there has been no such commitment from the biggest chains, Asda and Tesco being notably resistant to action.[20]

Climate change

Global climate change is possibly the biggest public policy challenge we face. Our economies are already having an impact on the climate; temperatures and sea levels are rising (average global temperatures are now warmer than at any time during the last 120,000 years), ice caps are melting and there has been an increase in the severity and frequency of extreme weather events such as droughts, floods and storms. Insurance claims relating to weather damage, for example, exceeded US$90 billion in 1998 alone, more than reported in the entire 1980s.[21]

This will increasingly have devastating impacts on the natural environment with species such as birds, mammals and insects trying to migrate as their local weather system becomes unsuitable. Others that cannot migrate, such as plants and trees, will start to disappear, creating further problems for the local ecosystems. In essence the weather conditions are changing too fast for the natural environment to adapt.

The cause is emissions of greenhouse gases from virtually all economic activity, with the main source of 'human-enhanced emissions' (ie produced by us) being carbon dioxide from energy use. Forum for the Future concludes that the globalisation of food-supply networks and their associated emissions have become a major concern and a hotly debated issue.[22]

Food miles

Global free trade allows supermarkets to play off farmers around the world against each other so that they can get the lowest price. This has caused international food trade to increase faster than the world's population and food production. According to Andy Jones's report 'Eating Oil', between 1968 and 1998, world food production increased by 84 per cent, population by 91 per cent and food trade by 184 per cent. Rather than importing what they cannot produce themselves, many countries appear to be simply 'swapping food'. In 1997, the UK imported 126 million litres of milk and exported 270 million litres.[23]

Long-distance transportation of food produces vast amounts of pollution, excess packaging and use of chemical preservatives, uses up large amounts of fossil fuels and thus contributes significantly to climate change.[24] We put in more energy (in the form of non-renewable fossil fuels) than we get out (in the form of food calories):[25]

- **The distribution of one kilogramme of apples from New Zealand sold in the UK accounts for its own weight in carbon dioxide emissions.[26]**

- **For every calorie of iceberg lettuce flown in from Los Angeles, we use 127 calories of fuel.[27]**

This is aided by the fact that there is no taxation on aviation fuel, making importing goods into the UK highly viable for supermarkets.[28] In November 2000 a motorist paid 80p for a litre of unleaded petrol, and airlines paid 18p for a litre of fuel.[29]

Andy Jones goes on to report that the organic sector seems to be repeating these trends, with UK imports of meat growing from 5 per cent of the market in 1998–89 to 30 per cent in 1999–2000. Of all organic food consumed in the UK, three-quarters is imported. This is because UK farmers, like their conventional counterparts, cannot always supply large volumes of standard produce all year round to the major retailers who dominate the distribution system.[28] One sample basket of 26 imported organic products could release as much carbon dioxide into the atmosphere as an average four-bedroom household does through cooking meals for eight months. The 26 products collectively could travel a distance equivalent to six times round the equator (241,000 kilometres) before they hit our shelves.[30]

The UK Cabinet Office reported that the food system accounts for up to 40 per cent of all UK road freight.[31] The overall UK freight market has grown 65 per cent in the last two decades, with the average length of haul now 95 miles. Road haulage accounts for 7 per cent of the UK's carbon dioxide emissions and, according to DEFRA, is the fastest-growing source of greenhouse gases.[32] The 'just-in-time' delivery system of centralised distribution, which sees products rushed to stores as and when they are needed, is another supermarket practice that impacts on the environment. Friends of the Earth state that Tesco's vehicles clocked up 224 million kilometres last year, Sainsbury's 115.7 million kilometres and Wal-Mart 147.9 million kilometres.[33]

The New Economics Foundation states that out-of-town superstores also cause transport congestion and pollution problems as people turn to cars to do their shopping. The distance travelled to shops increased by

60 per cent between 1975 and 1990, and now three quarters of supermarket customers travel by car.[34] Meanwhile, Friends of the Earth estimate that a typical out-of-town superstore causes £25,000 worth of air pollution and associated damage to the local community every week.[35]

The distances involved in the distribution of fresh produce can be demonstrated by looking at a traditional meal. If bought at a supermarket, many ingredients will have been imported and could have travelled, cumulatively, over 24,000 miles. However, choosing seasonal products and purchasing them locally at a farmers' market, for instance, could reduce the total distance to 376 miles – 66 times fewer food miles.[36] Unfortunately, the supermarkets do not typically source food locally, preferring central distribution networks that are easier to manage. The table below illustrates the carbon dioxide emissions from different forms of food transport.

If the UK government is serious about tackling climate change, it needs to address air travel: by supporting a Europe-wide tax on aviation fuel and informing consumers of food miles, and through a mandatory food labelling scheme showing the distance the food has travelled and the related carbon-dioxide emissions.

The carbon dioxide (CO_2) emissions of organic food sourcing, distribution and marketing systems (grams of CO_2 per kilogram product)[37]

	To Britain	To whole-sale/distri-bution centre	To store	To the home	Total CO_2
Imported: flown from Mexico. Bought at supermarket	Plane=5,069	Truck=13	Truck=6	Car=183	5,278
Imported: shipped from New Zealand. Bought at supermarket	Ship=230	Truck=13	Truck=6	Car=183	432
Imported: trucked from Sicily. Bought at supermarket	Truck=154	Truck=13	Truck=6	Car=183	356
Regional: trucked from regional area. Bought at independent			Truck=12	Car=183	195
Local: trucked from local area. Bought at **farmers' market**			Truck=4	Car=183	187
Local: produced locally. Bought at **farm shop**				Car=183	183
Local: produced locally. Delivered via **box scheme**				Van=17	17

Local sourcing

As a result of recent food scares, increased demand for local food and concern about food miles, there has been considerable pressure in the last two years for multiple supermarkets to source their products and services more locally. There are five perceived benefits associated with this, according to Vicky Hird and Merav Shub from Sustain: [38]

1. To renew the relationship between producer and consumer.

2. To strengthen local economies and reduce 'leakage' of both finance and other resources (including labour and nutrients) from the local economy.

3. To create opportunities for more secure and sustainable food supplies.

4. To improve relationships with local authorities and citizens, eg to facilitate planning decisions.

5. To reduce the environmental impact of complex, lengthy distribution patterns of food.

Yet the larger retailers argue that the typical centralised system of delivery that they use is vital to operating due diligence and achieving the required volumes and quality control. In general, store managers of the multiples are not responsible for orders and have no control over local supply; although in some cases they are able to suggest local suppliers they would like to use, who are then subject to central management and procedures.[39]

Food supplies from the surrounding area, often referred to as 'local food links', have however been gaining a small market share. Vegetable and fruit box delivery schemes, direct mail and delivery schemes, community-supported agriculture, farmers' markets, and initiatives such as consumer-buying co-operatives are all becoming more popular, and studies in the UK and the US suggest that increasing such initiatives would have a positive local economic and environmental impact.[40]

The last two years have seen a plethora of policy announcements and initiatives by the main supermarket chains on local sourcing; but much of this seems to be rhetoric.[41] A recent survey found that the top 10 super-markets recognised local food as a sector with potential and most wanted to increase the amount of locally and regionally produced food lines they sold. Some had targets in place. However, food from clearly identifiable but large regions such as Wales, Scotland and Northern Ireland, and to a lesser extent the south west and south east, dominates much of what supermarkets consider 'local food'.[42]

The ideal supermarket, according to Sustain, would provide a window on local agriculture by achieving high levels of support for regional foods and local economies. Given the huge educational role supermarkets now play, initiatives and promotions can help generate increased consumer awareness of local producers.[43] According to the Cabinet Office, over 90 per cent of consumers want to know where the meat in their pork pie or sausages comes from and they need access to well-presented, accurate information and guidance about the food they are buying from these areas. There are some useful leaflets available, such as Tesco's 'Local' leaflet, but in-store promotions of local produce are infrequent.[44] There is, however, an increasing commitment shown by the major stores, in particular Sainsbury's, to label county of origin and farm addresses, mainly on 'speciality' foods such as cheese.

However, Asda, which at least has a policy on local sourcing, is still only aiming for a modest 2 per cent of turnover from locally sourced goods. In contrast, a survey by the Green Party in Ludlow found that 81 per cent of town-centre food shops and market traders sold some local produce, and 55 per cent of these sold more than 70 per cent local produce.[45]

The small, northern supermarket chain Booths has done much on local sourcing, according to Sustain:[46]

- **Promotions are often based on regional foods, stressing the provenance, variety and quality of regional foods.**

- **Booths has a large supplier base in order to maintain choice for the company and for customers, and has built up strong links between buyers and suppliers. Some buyers have been working in the same product area for many years.**

- **The effort Booths makes in promoting regional produce is significant, and they see this as a key element in their promotions and marketing strategy. As with other multiples, few lines are supplied direct from suppliers to store; however the company does source 20–25 per cent of produce from the four counties referred to above.**

In addition to local sourcing of products, supermarkets should have a policy of using businesses (eg banking, legal, cleaning and maintenance, utilities, printing and publicity) local to their stores where possible. Supermarkets' highly controlled and centralised decision-making processes mean that all stores tend to employ the same companies for the bulk of these services. Research shows that a new supermarket means job losses and deskilling of the local employment pool. If the decision-making process was decentralised to individual stores, then each store's managers could choose to use local financial and other services, thereby supporting the local economy.[47]

Local sourcing has two main advantages in that it cuts down on transport and helps small producers sell their products at a fair price to the local community. Supermarkets have a role to play but could destroy these advantages by transporting produce to central depots and using their buying pressure to push down producers' profits. The key is to have a diversity of food retailers, resulting in real competition, with food markets selling local produce on the one hand, and supermarkets sourcing local products on the other.

Animal welfare

In a revealing report to the International Institute for Environment and Development, Philip Lymbery from Compassion in World Farming states that intensive agriculture in Europe and America has caused many problems for the farming industry. These include serious disease problems, a diminished environment, poor welfare in farm animals and threats to farming communities and rural livelihoods. There is now serious debate in Europe on charting a course towards a sustainable agricultural system that, to be successful, must also pay full regard to animal welfare.[48]

The latter half of the last century saw the rapid rise of factory farming in Western Europe and the US; characterised by large numbers of farm animals being caged or crated, and crammed into windowless sheds. According to animal welfare charity Compassion in World Farming, three classic factory-farm methods of the 1960s epitomise this approach; veal crates for calves, stall and tether-cages for pregnant pigs and battery cages for laying hens.[49] There has now been an awakening in Europe to the fact that animals are sentient beings, capable of feeling pain and suffering, and the European Union (EU) has now outlawed the above methods.[50]

However, factory farming in the 1980s and 1990s continued to expand in more insidious forms. Factory farming has concentrated on intensifying its breeding and feeding regimes, making animals grow faster or produce more milk, with devastating consequences for the animals concerned. Broiler chickens that are crippled or suffer heart attacks before the age of six weeks, and dairy cows with a metabolic system that can scarcely keep pace with their over-producing udders are just two examples. The new breed of factory farm has intensified the physiological strain put on the animals, while at the same time rearing animals in ever-larger groups and at high stocking densities (more animals per acre).[51]

Compassion in World Farming states that Europe is now counting the cost of its intensive farming methods. The clean-up cost of foot-and-mouth disease (FMD) in the UK is estimated at £15–30 billion.[52] Excessive animal transport can exacerbate disease problems through poor welfare and mixing of animals. Classical swine fever and FMD and are recent examples of diseases transmitted when animals were transported. When animal welfare is jeopardised, food safety, too, is compromised. Bovine Spongiform Encephalopathy (BSE), or 'mad cow disease', resulted from turning natural herbivores – cattle – into carnivores by feeding them meat and bone meal. Over 100 people have contracted the fatal human equivalent of BSE in the UK, and by 1996, BSE had cost the UK £288 million. Food poisoning epidemics such as salmonella and Campylobacter in eggs and poultry meat cost the UK £350 million per year. In the US, where livestock farming is often even more intensive, food poisoning is four times more common.[53]

Yet supermarkets can have enormous influence over animal welfare standards. Supermarkets represent the main conduit by which low-welfare animal products reach the general public. Their huge buying power means they can move quickly and decisively – perhaps

more so than political decision-makers[54] – on food standards issues including animal welfare. The vast majority
of fresh animal produce in major supermarkets is sold
under company-own labels, where they have direct
control over how the animals are reared and slaughtered.
Supermarkets also have tremendous scope for promoting
one product over another. According to Compassion In
World Farming, methods such as price promotions,
labelling, in-store positioning and customer information
can all be used to promote ethically reared food, and
there is a growing recognition amongst major retailers
that animal welfare is a key part of corporate responsibility.[55]

So what would the perfect welfare-friendly supermarket look like? Compassion in World Farming has
developed the following points:[56]

1. All red meat, poultry meat, milk and eggs
   would be free range or organically produced,
   including all fresh and processed produce
   and all manufactured foods and ready-made
   meals containing animal products as an
   ingredient. This would extend to the
   company's entire range of branded products
   as well as its own-label range.

2. A transitional requirement would be that all
   intensively produced animal products would
   be clearly labelled according to method of
   farm production.

3. No fish products would come from intensive farms. Only organically produced or wild fish would be sold. None of the animals reared for the supermarkets would have been subjected to mutilations such as tail docking, teeth clipping, debeaking or castration.

4. No products from genetically engineered strains of animals would be accepted, nor those produced using genetically modified production enhancers such as Bovine Somatotropin (BST) for dairy cows.

5. No animals or meat would be accepted from livestock subjected to livestock-auction markets. Journey times for animals travelling to slaughter would be reduced and ultimately animals would be slaughtered on the farm of rearing or the local abattoir.

6. No exotic animal products would be sold that are produced from essentially wild animals or those where production imposes severe welfare problems. Examples here include ostrich and emu meat, frogs' legs and foie gras.

7. The supermarket should have a written animal-welfare policy with targets that are reviewed annually.

8. **A main Board or Executive member should be appointed with specific responsibility for animal welfare. In addition, a dedicated animal-welfare officer should be appointed to the staff to implement the company's animal-welfare policy.**

The Department for Environment, Food and Rural Affairs (DEFRA) states that there is growing demand for food produced to higher standards of animal welfare. Certain consumers are willing to pay a premium for food produced to more welfare-friendly standards. 'Assured' products have increasingly been branded as such, for example through the red tractor logo that specifies legal minimum requirements for animal welfare. The Freedom Food scheme set up by the Royalty Society for the Prevention of Cruelty to Animals (RSPCA) in 1994 is another good example; farms affiliated to this scheme are inspected regularly to see that they meet five basic 'freedoms': the freedom from fear and distress, from hunger and thirst, from discomfort, from pain, injury and disease and the freedom to express normal behaviour. Just under 2,500 farms are currently members.[57]

According to DEFRA, consumers will buy particular foods for a variety of reasons, including quality (such as 'corn fed' or 'organic'), the expected taste, or the welfare conditions under which the food is produced. The consumption of free-range eggs, for example, has increased from 8 per cent in 1992 to around 22 per cent currently. The premium – nearly double – that consumers pay for free-range eggs over what they pay for battery eggs provides an indication of the value they assign animal welfare, alongside other perceived benefits.[58]

A number of supermarkets say that they are committed to upholding and improving the standards of animal welfare across all the products they sell and some now sell only free-range eggs.[59] For example, the Co-operative Group label battery-produced eggs as 'From Caged Hens' rather than the misleading label of 'Farm Fresh' commonly used in the industry. Marks and Spencer have gone a step further by selling only free-range eggs and only using free-range eggs as ingredients in all their products, such as quiches, pasta and biscuits. The willingness of consumers to pay a premium for organically produced meat may also be partly due to their perception that organic systems are more welfare friendly.

Fish

The environmental impact of supermarkets also extends to fish. Many of the world's marine fisheries are currently overexploited or have unacceptable impacts on the wider environment, according to the RSPB. Globally, more than 60 per cent of marine fisheries are fully or over-exploited. In 1992, one of the world's richest cod fisheries, the Great Banks off the Newfoundland coast, was virtually wiped out by over-fishing. Not only was the marine environment severely damaged, but some 40,000 jobs were lost. In the North East Atlantic, 40 of the 60 main commercial fish stocks, including all nine species listed for the North Sea, are believed to be 'outside safe biological limits'. This means that 67 per cent of stocks are seriously depleted or in danger of becoming so. Current fishing practices are not only threatening the sustainability of fish stocks, but having a significant impact on other wildlife, by using nets that also catch albatross, sea turtle and dolphin.[60]

Supermarkets currently source seafood products from all over the world, and it is a major challenge to establish whether the species they are sourcing and the fisheries that supply these species are sustainable and well managed.[61] According to the RSPB, it is now a legal requirement that most fish products for sale must indicate: [62]

- **The commercial names of the species.**

- **Information on the method of production such as 'caught at sea', 'caught in fresh water', or 'farmed or cultivated'.**

- **Where the seafood was caught or in the case of products caught in freshwater or farmed, the member state or third country of origin.**

The Marine Stewardship Council (MSC) is an independent, global, non-profit organisation based in London. In a bid to reverse the decline in the world's fisheries, the MSC is seeking to harness consumer purchasing power to generate change and promote environmentally responsible stewardship of one of the world's most important renewable food source. Its aims are:[63]

- To increase the overall sustainability of the world's seafood supply.

- To increase the percentage of the global seafood market certified to the MSC Standard.

- To increase awareness of the MSC eco-label (see below).

The MSC label[64]

Though operating independently since 1999, the MSC was first established by Unilever, the world's largest buyer of seafood, and the conservation charity WWF-UK, the international conservation organisation, in 1997.[65] It has developed an environmental standard for sustainable and well-managed fisheries and uses a product label to reward environmentally responsible fishery management and practices. Consumers will increasingly be able to choose seafood products that are labelled to prove the product has not contributed to over-fishing.

The verdict

The response within the supermarket industry to environmental challenges and the level and commitment to reporting is varied. According to Forum for the Future, while some supermarkets have environmental management systems (including environmental issues and aspects of performance in their annual report and producing environmental reports) others do not. The quality of reporting also varies considerably, with several companies still limiting their reports to a discussion of the issues and highlighting success stories but failing to implement meaningful performance targets.[66]

If supermarkets do participate in voluntary initiatives, such as the farm-assurance scheme, they should still expect to be held to account. For example, Tesco has been expelled from the prestigious '95+ Group', an influential ethical trading initiative run by WWF-UK, after refusing to give written assurances that it would stop selling illegally felled wood from Indonesian rainforests.[67]

And fines being levied on supermarkets for abuse of the environment suggests that supermarkets are still guilty of causing a significant negative impact on the environment, both directly and where their influence has caused others to damage the environment. The Environment Agency (the environmental regulator for England and Wales) fined Tesco £10,000 in court after 6,000 litres of petrol leaked from its Tower Park store in Dorset over six months, polluting groundwater. Tesco was also fined £30,000 in 2001 for permitting the dumping of more than 30 shopping trolleys in the River Chelmer in Chelmsford, Essex. And Budgens was fined

£16,000 after staff at its Tadley store poured dairy products down the drain when chillers and freezers broke down; milk 'devastated' a local stream.[68]

Environmental fines in the UK are tiny in comparison to the profits large companies such as supermarkets produce each year. These small fines cannot deter companies from breaking the law in the future unless it affects their public image. However, they also show that supermarkets are entering the realms usually reserved for the more heavily polluting industries such as power stations.

But many of the issues raised here, of course, are not solely the consequence of the actions of just supermarkets. Consumers purchase the products, government fails to control through legislation and tax and other industries must bear responsibility as well. Even so, supermarkets through their size and sheer power should be held primarily accountable for this environmental destruction. Supermarkets have some awareness of their roles and have implemented various environmental initiatives such as Sainsbury's green store and Co-op's biodegradable plastic carrier bags (see below). These are welcome but are either one-off or small initiatives that have not been introduced to all products and activities. Supermarkets need to recognise that their activities have environmental consequence far greater than they may wish to acknowledge. Supermarkets, consumers and the government need to take responsibility for these environmental impacts and work together as well as separately to reduce or eliminate them.

Sainsbury's 'green' store [69]

Sainsbury's Greenwich store, which opened in 1999, provided an ideal opportunity to trial designs for improved energy efficiency, and to test new technologies and approaches. Sainsbury's are using the lessons learnt from this project in new stores and to develop other initiatives.

Initiatives in the Greenwich store include:

- Earth-banked sides to insulate the store and reduce visual impact.

- North-facing double-glazed roof lights to maximise the use of natural daylight.

- Thermal blinds to reduce heat loss and light pollution.

- Underfloor heating to maximise the natural tendency of hot air to rise.

- Water, drawn from boreholes in the chalk aquifer at a constant 10°C to cool the building in hot weather.

- Wind and solar power to provide energy for store entrance signs and the electric-car charging point.

- A Combined Heat and Power plant using gas to provide electricity.

- Recycled matting in the foyer made from aircraft tyres.

- Forest Stewardship Council certified wooden fascia panels on the store exterior.

- Splashbacks in the customer toilets made from recycled plastic and yoghurt pots.

The Co-op's biodegradable plastic carrier bag [70]

The Co-op is the first British grocery retailer to use degradable carrier bags, supplied by Symphony Plastic Technologies. These bags are 100 per cent degradable, but are still as strong as non-degradable carrier bags and can still be reused. The bags will be date marked, and from the date of manufacture the plastic will start to degrade in approximately 18 months time, taking 3 years. This process may speed up if the bags are exposed to sunlight and/or heat.

The Co-op degradable carrier bag degrades completely, leaving only carbon dioxide, water and a small amount of mineralisation compatible with soil. The bags do not leave any toxic elements in the environment. In landfill situations, the bag will still degrade and therefore help to reduce the amount of dangerous methane gas that can build up when normal plastic bags stay intact with waste inside.

As the bags break down into smaller particles, they are degraded by natural microbic activity. They do not need compost or any other form of biological activity to break down, but if they are put on a compost heap* or similar environment they will become biodegradable.

The Co-op recognises that this technology does not contribute to reducing the total amount of plastic carrier bags used, but believes that until other ways of positively encouraging consumers to use less plastics are implemented, this new technology offers a step change that will help to reduce long-term littering. It is estimated that the average life of a single, giveaway carrier bag is only 3 minutes before being discarded. The UK grocery industry uses enough carrier bags to carpet the entire planet twice a year (source IGD) and, according to government figures, each person on average uses 134 bags a year, which in England is equivalent to 323 bags per household.

(*Industrial compost is typically maintained at above 55°C. Any less than that, such as in garden compost heaps, and sometimes even leaves and grass cuttings will not break down.)

Chapter 5

Supermarket Food

Consumers and small businesses, farmers and workers, animal welfare and the environment are all losers in the supermarkets' aggressive pursuit of cheap food. The endless search for the cheapest product from around the globe involves putting small farmers out of business, putting low quality food on our shelves, and damaging the environment, because food is travelling further and farmers are unable to invest in sustainable methods of production. And are consumers really benefiting when what they are getting is lower quality, less choice, and the cheapest deals on unhealthy products? For fresh produce, supermarkets are often more expensive than the local greengrocer or market they would like to close down. And when the global giants such as Tesco and Wal-Mart have destroyed the local competition, you can be sure that they will put their prices back up.

Sandra Bell, Food and Farming Campaigner,
Friends of the Earth, 30/01/04

In the UK it has been estimated that half the food consumed by 57 million mouths is bought from just 1,000 stores. In 1996, 35 per cent of the £118 billion spent on food went as profit to the retail sector.[1] The illustration below shows how much different areas of the food-supply chain contribute to the UK economy.

This chapter explains how the supermarkets' power affects the food we eat; from pesticide-ridden fresh produce, organic produce that is over-packaged and imported, through to unhealthy microwavable ready-meals, limited choice and high-fat, -sugar and -salt foods targeted at our children. But there is hope; this chapter concludes with ways we can change the food system.

The cost of cheap supermarket food

According to the *Ecologist*, if we did our sums correctly we would know that the high yields of intensive farming come at a cost of soil degradation, carbon loss into the atmosphere, pesticide and fertiliser run-off into our water-ways and, most pernicious of all, food products that are positively unhealthy. As Professor Jules Pretty of the University of Essex has shown, the external costs of inten-sive farming in the UK amount to as much as £208 per hectare. The water companies, for instance, pay up to £135 million a year to ensure that drinking water complies with European Union pesticide limits; all in all we may be paying as much as £2 billion a year for the environ-mental and health costs of UK agriculture. The irony is that not only do the intensive farmers go scot-free, but they receive up to £3 billion per year in direct subsidies.[2]

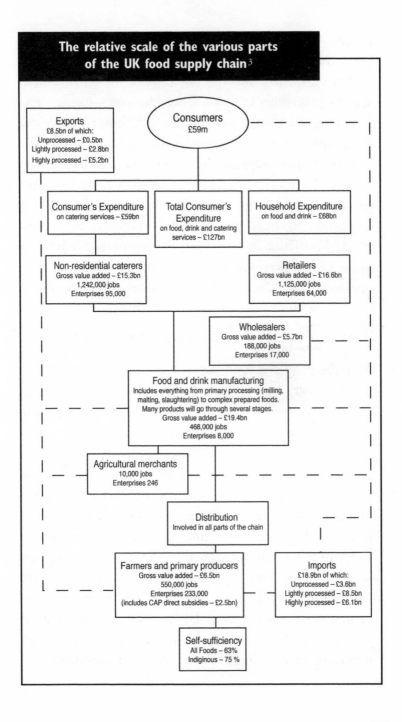

The relative scale of the various parts of the UK food supply chain[3]

Exports
£8.5bn of which:
Unprocessed – £0.5bn
Lightly processed – £2.8bn
Highly processed – £5.2bn

Consumers
£59m

Consumer's Expenditure
on catering services – £59bn

Total Consumer's Expenditure
on food, drink and catering services – £127bn

Household Expenditure
on food and drink – £68bn

Non-residential caterers
Gross value added – £15.3bn
1,242,000 jobs
Enterprises 95,000

Retailers
Gross value added – £16.6bn
1,125,000 jobs
Enterprises 64,000

Wholesalers
Gross value added – £5.7bn
188,000 jobs
Enterprises 17,000

Food and drink manufacturing
Includes everything from primary processing (milling, malting, slaughtering) to complex prepared foods. Many products will go through several stages.
Gross value added – £19.4bn
468,000 jobs
Enterprises 8,000

Agricultural merchants
10,000 jobs
Enterprises 246

Distribution
Involved in all parts of the chain

Farmers and primary producers
Gross value added – £6.5bn
550,000 jobs
Enterprises 233,000
(includes CAP direct subsidies – £2.5bn)

Imports
£18.9bn of which:
Unprocessed – £3.6bn
Lightly processed – £8.5bn
Highly processed – £6.1bn

Self-sufficiency
All Foods – 63%
Indiginous – 75 %

Inevitably, maintains the *Ecologist*, those producers and small processors who either do not want, or are unable to comply with the supermarkets will find themselves increasingly cut out of the main retailing market. Constantly battling to expand their interests at the expense of each other through the price war, the big retailers need a global market for purchasing their goods. Here we have a classic situation in which producers who apply strict environmental and health standards are likely to lose out to those who do not. Some economists now question whether, in the light of globalisation, the US needs its farmers. The same also applies to the UK.[4]

Cheap food has resulted in industrial agriculture, ie large companies running enormous farms. The benefits of industrial agriculture have been marketed to society, but the box below shows that these are false, exposing the dangers of the food we eat.

Seven deadly myths of industrial agriculture[5]

Myth One: industrial agriculture will feed the world
Truth: world hunger is not created by lack of food but by poverty and landlessness, which deny people access to food. Industrial agriculture actually increases hunger by raising the cost of farming; by forcing tens of millions of farmers off the land, and by growing primarily high-profit export and luxury crops.[6]

Myth Two: industrial food is safe, healthy and nutritious
Truth: industrial agriculture contaminates our vegetables and fruits with pesticides, slips dangerous bacteria into our lettuce and puts genetically engineered growth hormones into our milk. It is not surprising that cancer, food-borne illnesses, and obesity are at an all-time high.[7]

Myth Three: industrial food is cheap
Truth: if you add the real cost of industrial food – its health, environmental, and social costs – to the current supermarket price, not even our wealthiest citizens could afford to buy it.[8]

Myth Four: industrial agriculture is efficient
Truth: small farms produce more agricultural output per unit area than large farms. Moreover, larger, less diverse farms require far more mechanical and chemical inputs. These ever-increasing inputs are devastating to the environment and make these farms far less efficient than smaller, more sustainable farms.[9]

Myth Five: industrial food offers more choice
Truth: the supermarkets give an illusion of choice. Food labelling does not even tell us what pesticides are on our food or what products have been genetically engineered. Most importantly, the myth of choice masks the tragic loss of tens of thousands of crop varieties caused by industrial agriculture.[10]

Myth Six: industrial agriculture benefits the environment and wildlife
Truth: industrial agriculture is the largest single threat to the earth's biodiversity. Fence-row-to-fence-row ploughing, planting, and harvesting techniques decimate wildlife habitats, while massive chemical use poisons the soil and water, and kills off countless plant and animal communities.[11]

Myth Seven: biotechnology will solve the problems of industrial agriculture
Truth: new biotech crops will not solve industrial agriculture's problems, but will compound them and consolidate control of the world's food supply in the hands of a few large corporations. Biotechnology will destroy biodiversity and food security, and drive self-sufficient farmers off their land.[12]

Pesticides

One side-effect of the perfect-looking fruit and vegetables we see in the supermarket aisles is the pesticide residues left by them; not only do pesticides harm the environment, as already discussed, there is evidence that this has detrimental consequences for our health. Dr Vyvyan Howard, a leading toxicologist at the University of Liverpool, has studied the effects of pesticide combinations on unborn children and reports:

> *Pregnant women are now exposed to*
> *completely novel molecules that their*

grandmothers were not. Quite a number
of these are capable of hormone disruption
and various scientists' work shows that it
takes only extremely low doses to cause
effects. [13]

For example, the cocktail effect (the combination of pesticides) could be related to the decreased age of puberty in girls, which is known to have implications for breast cancer later (and the incidence of breast cancer has risen dramatically since the 1960s). 'This could be due to the imprinting of chemical disrupters in the womb,' Dr Howard says. He recommends buying organic. [14]

Supermarkets could do more to reduce pesticide use. Friends of the Earth suggest the codes of practice the multiples set up with farmers should aim for a significant reduction in pesticide use, with zero residues of pesticides in the food we eat. In practice, this means that there should be no detectable residues even as technology develops and allows lower and lower levels to be found. Supermarkets should also prohibit the use of pesticides that have the highest risk to the environment or health, such as carbendazim, lindane and vinclozolin, which disrupt the hormone system, and aldicarb and chlorpyrifos, which affect the nervous system. [15]

Farmers who supply the major supermarkets are normally required to follow protocols on pesticide use and these may suggest nonchemical ways of controlling pests and diseases. The most common of these are the 'assured produce' schemes, and we can see labelling to this effect on certain items of food in the shelves. However, there is so far little indication that these protocols have resulted in any notable decrease in pesticide use or residues in supermarket food. The table below shows the residue levels in supermarket fruit and vegetables according to the Pesticide Residues Committee (PRC).[16]

Pesticide residues in supermarket food 1998–2001[17]

Supermarket residue	% fruit and veg with
Somerfield	60
Safeway	49
Marks and Spencer	49
Tesco	48
Sainsbury's	48
Asda	48
Waitrose	46
Co-op	43
Morrisons	42

Organic food

The latest trend in the supermarkets is organic food; briefly put, food that is produced without pesticides and fertilisers, and livestock farming that doesn't routinely use antibiotics or hormones and looks after the animals' welfare. The Soil Association provides the standards for organic food and farming in the UK. Below is a more detailed look at organic farming methods.

Key elements of organic farming [18]

The main components of an organic farming system are the avoidance of artificial fertilisers and pesticides, the use of crop rotations and other forms of husbandry to maintain fertility and control weeds, pests and diseases. The management of organic livestock, soil and crops requires special care in nurturing positive health and vitality.

Rotations

A correctly designed and implemented crop rotation is at the core of organic crop production. The rotation contains the following key elements:

- Provides sufficient crop nutrients and minimises their losses.
- Provides nitrogen through leguminous crops.
- Aims to control weeds, pests and diseases.
- Maintains the soil structure and organic matter content.
- Provides a profitable output of organic cash crops and/or livestock.

Fertility is generally provided by animal manure and leguminous nitrogen. The aim of the organic system is to be self-sustaining, although in some instances one can bring in organic fertilisers or mineral products such as rock phosphate.

Crop protection

No synthetic products can be used in organic farming although, where direct intervention is required, non-synthetic substances such as sulphur, and biological pest controls may be used. Pest, weed and disease control are achieved through the rotation, choice of varieties, timing of cultivations and habitat management to encourage natural predators.

Livestock

Livestock forms an integral part of the majority of organic farms. Usually they are supported by the farm's own resources and are land based; ie no intensively housed stock or systems where a large amount of the total feed has to be bought in and manure disposed of away from the farm. Most existing dairy, beef and sheep enterprises can be converted to an organic system, given the appropriate changes to feeding and housing. Pigs and poultry are managed extensively under an organic system, with outdoor access.

Soil Association organic standards require that the ratio is between 70 per cent and 90 per cent organic and that for ruminants at least 60 per cent of dry matter is from fresh or conserved forage. The aim is to maintain closed flocks and herds, and to breed and rear all replacements, although it is possible to buy in up to 10 per cent a year. All animals slaughtered for meat must be born and raised on an organic holding, so calves or stores bought in from a conventional farm cannot be sold as organic.

Animal health

Animal health within organic systems relies on preventative management and good husbandry. Routine use of antibiotics, wormers and vaccines is not permitted, although particular products are allowed where there is a known farm problem. Conventional medicines can be used where it is necessary to prevent prolonged illness or suffering, and increased withdrawal periods for all medicines are required. The use of homeopathy is encouraged.

The Soil Association's organic symbol

The Soil Association's organic symbol is the UK's largest and most recognisable trademark for organic produce. Wherever you see it you can be sure that the food you have purchased has been produced and processed to the Soil Association's strict and rigorous animal welfare and environmental standards.

According to the Soil Association in 2003[19] :

1. Demand for organic food increased by 55 per cent between 1999 and 2000 and one-third between 2000 and 2001. The UK market is currently worth over £920 million.

2. There are 3,865 organic farmers (including around 600 in Wales, 700 in Scotland and 100 in Northern Ireland). There are 2,000 food-processing facilities that can handle organic food separately from non-organic in the UK.

3. The amount of organic land in the UK almost doubled between April 2001 and 2002, and is equivalent to three times the size of Greater London.

There are criticisms of the supermarkets overselling organic food for a large profit, using excess packaging and getting their supplies from overseas – adding to food miles – even though UK-produced supplies are often readily available. A survey by Friends of the Earth in 2002 found that:[20]

1. Overall, 70 per cent of organic food sold in the UK is currently imported.

2. There is a large increase in the number of lines but most is packaged and imported.

3. Tesco, the UK's largest food-retailer, sources a massive 80 per cent of its organic produce from overseas.

4. Best performers are Waitrose, who currently source 85 per cent of its organic produce from the UK. Marks and Spencer also do well with 60 per cent coming from UK sources.

GM food

Genetically Modified (GM) food is a huge issue for farmers, supermarkets, consumers and the UK government. There have been consumer-led resistance against farm trials in Europe and the UK but pilots have gone ahead. GM food is a real concern to the public and so far the supermarkets still keep it off their shelves, but this could change if public opinion does not remain strongly opposed to this new technology. The government, largely supportive of encouraging the growth of the biotechnology industry in this area, organised a public debate in 2003 in an effort to promote GM food. The following extract summaries information provided to the public on GM food during the debate:

**Information on GM from the UK Government's
GM Nation Public Debate in 2003**[21]

What is GM?

**Genetic Modification (GM) involves moving genetic material
from the cells of one organism to those of another, be they
related or unrelated.**

Views for:

- GM provides a valuable new tool, for example, in plant breeding.

- GM makes it possible to move genes into new crop varieties to make significant and targeted improvements (eg insect or disease resistance) where this is difficult or impossible by traditional plant breeding. GM is possible because DNA and the way that genes work are universal.

Views against:

- A scientific definition alone cannot convey the real meaning of GM and the way it is being applied.

- GM marks a radical departure in our use of living things for commercial purposes, and a fundamentally different way of breeding plants and animals. The greatest concerns arise when GM involves crossing species barriers, creating organisms that would never arise in nature, to be used for industrial purposes in the wider environment.

Where and how is GM done?

GM is initially a laboratory process. A common soil bacterium that naturally transfers genes into plant cells is the preferred method for producing new GM crops, although there are other techniques. Isolated cells or tissues from the plant are treated with the bacterium containing the new genes. The bacteria are then removed and plants grown from cells containing the new genes.

Views for:

- Regulatory authorities require companies producing GM plants to submit scientific evidence for the exact changes produced, as part of the package of information required for product approval.

- The genes used in the modification are identified with molecular precision using a wide range of biotechnological methods. A large number of new GM plants are produced and then tested and selected over several generations to identify particular plants that show only the desired effect. These plants must also exhibit an absence of 'side effects', and must show stable inheritance of the new gene from one generation to the next.

- GM crops are more thoroughly tested and evaluated than those from traditional plant breeding programmes. GM crops have been tested since the early 1980s in many hundreds of trials and are now grown on nearly 60 million hectares around the world annually. They have performed as expected and have been widely adopted by farmers in both developed and resource-poor countries.

Views against:

- There is little control on where the gene inserts itself into the host DNA. Scientists have shown that a gene's position in relation to other genes has an effect on what it does, therefore GM may lead to unpredictable and possibly harmful results.

- Scientists do not know enough about gene interactions to prevent such harmful effects occurring, and laboratory testing may not detect all changes.

- The effects of releasing genetically modified organisms into the environment could be unpredictable. GM crops have only been released into the environment on a large scale in the last several years. No one knows at this stage what will be the long-term effects.

What GM foods are available?

Currently, food ingredients from varieties of GM soya, maize and oilseed rape have been approved for food use in the European Union, although very little is actually used. No fresh GM produce has been approved for sale or consumption in the UK.

Elsewhere, dozens of GM food crops have been approved for growing and use in at least one of the 16 countries that have commercialised GM crops.

Views for:

- The majority of processed foods in the US, Canada, Japan and Argentina, and increasingly in other countries, include GM ingredients.

Views against:

- The current UK voluntary agreement, limiting the commecial growing of GM crops in the UK, plus the labelling of GM-derived ingredients in food, has come largely in response to public pressure led by high-profile campaigns.

- Public rejection of GM has led most UK food retailers to remove GM products and foods with GM ingredients from their own-brand products.

What about new GM products?

People disagree whether the wide range of possible new crops will either be successfully grown, or bring the benefits claimed.

Views for:

- Biotechnology researchers are working to develop GM crops that will bring commercial, agricultural and health benefits. A wide variety of new crops in development aim to increase pest and disease resistance, improve food value and provide other commercially useful benefits.

- GM crops aim to help producers to increase their yields whilst reducing inputs. This is of course especially helpful in developing countries.

- GM products such as Golden Rice and Golden Mustard are being developed that are enriched with beta-carotene, which humans convert to vitamin A. This could help in the fight against vitamin A deficiency, which can lead to blindness in developing countries.

- Research is also being carried out into GM crops with higher levels of nutrients, such as iron, zinc and calcium, to help reduce dietary deficiencies.

- GM technology can also help to reduce allergens such as those found in peanuts or wheat.

- Other GM crops in development include products with increased levels of phytonutrients, that can lower blood cholesterol levels, or remove anti-nutrients, which can cause negative health effects.

Views against:

- Many claims by the biotechnology industry about the future are unsubstantiated, as few experimental GM crops are succeeding – because their development is proving much more difficult than was imagined.

- GM companies have promised a variety of new products for many years such as rice with more vitamins and fruit that will rot more slowly, but they are either far from being commercially grown or have been withdrawn.

- Non-GM plant breeding could bring similar benefits without the hazards. Many of the 'improvements' associated with these GM crops, such as salt tolerance and increased vitamin content, may be obtained through traditional breeding methods.

- Others may prove too difficult to manage in the field. There are already examples of problems, e.g. when GM-pharmaceutical-crop residues contaminated a non-GM food crop in the USA.

The conclusions from the GM debate were:[22]

1. People are generally uneasy about GM.

2. The more people engage in GM issues, the more resolved their attitudes and more intense their concerns.

3. There is little support for early commercialisation.

4. There is widespread mistrust of government and multi-national companies.

5. There is a broad desire to know more and for further research to be done.

6. Developing countries are a special case because they could benefit more than the UK from, for example, GM crops with increased pest and disease resistance.

The US government, bending to pressure from agribusiness, has never required labels to inform consumers about the pesticides and other chemicals used on crops or the residues still left on those foods at time of purchase.[23] After a five-year moratorium on new GM foods, the European Union allowed new GM products to be sold in Europe in December 2003. All GM food sold in the EU is identified with a specific label.[24] UK Supermarkets still ban genetically modified food ingredients in their own-brand products, despite pressure from the government to remove the ban.

Lack of choice

A persistent myth created by food manufacturers is that industrial production provides consumers with an extraordinary variety of food choices. According to Andrew Kimbrell in his book *The Fatal Harvest Reader*, industrial farming and processing, so the belief goes, have broken down limitations on food choices imposed by growing seasons, plants' geographical ranges and crop failures.[25] Kimbrell explains that wandering the aisles of a 40,000-square-foot superstore, we may be readily taken in by the myth; the breakfast cereal section, for example, may contain upwards of 50 different brand names, each uniquely packaged and presented. Take a minute, however, to try to find a variety made of a grain other than corn, rice, wheat or oats. For an equally daunting challenge, try to find a box that does not list sugar and salt among its leading ingredients.[26]

Each year, more than 15,000 new food introductions go on sale in the US. Clever marketing ploys and millions of dollars spent on packaging create a variety of images, graphics and materials to display these products in stores. However, these 'new products' rarely represent an increase in food choices for consumers; the packaging attempts to hide the fact that we are essentially eating the same ingredients over and over, even though they go by different names; 95 per cent of the calories we eat come from only 30 varieties of plants.[27]

A seldom-mentioned impact of industrial agriculture is that it deprives consumers of real choice by favouring only a few varieties of crops that allow efficient harvesting, processing and packaging.[28] There are over 2,500 national varieties of apple and 550 varieties of pear in the UK, many of which are commercially available to the supermarkets, who could stock them more often; apples such as Discovery, Cox, Gala, Spartan and Russet, and pears such as Concorde, Conference and Comice. A survey by Friends of the Earth in 2003 showed that supermarkets were sourcing on average only 40 per cent of their apples from the UK at the height of the British apple season. Greengrocers and market stalls managed to source more from the UK and, although the supermarkets did offer a wider variety of apple types, this was mainly due to imported varieties from Australia, New Zealand and the US. Yet 84 per cent of shoppers say they want supermarkets to give preference to British produce when it is in season.[29]

The supermarkets could do more to support our orchards. Traditional orchards form an important part of our cultural heritage and landscape, from the Somerset cider orchards that cling to the higher ground above the Somerset Levels to the cherry orchards that define the landscape of North Kent. The seasonal change of blossom, fruit, leaf-fall and winter dormancy are reflected in pruning, harvesting and wassailing; all distinctive to their locality. The orchards also support a wide variety of flora and fauna, such as woodpeckers, little owls, bats, butterflies, lichens, wild flowers and invertebrates such as the stag and cardinal beetles.[30]

Unfortunately, many orchards been grubbed out or replanted with low-growing bush trees, which are easier to spray and harvest mechanically. As this standardisation of production has increased, the traditional varieties of apples, pears and soft fruit have declined, driven by the desire by many supermarkets and consumers for fruit that is cheap, even sized, blemish-free, with good keeping qualities and all-year-round availability. Changing consumer taste in favour of sweeter varieties have also played a part.[31] It is true that without industrial processes we might not be able to eat a 'fresh' Red Delicious apple 365 days a year. However, consumers would be able to enjoy many of the thousands of apple varieties grown in the UK during the last century that have now all but disappeared. Because of the industrial agriculture system, the majority of those varieties are extinct today; just two varieties, Golden and Red Delicious, account for more than 50 per cent of the current apple market.[32] The monoculture of industrial agriculture has similarly reduced the natural diversity of nearly every other UK major food crop in terms of varieties grown, colour, size and flavour.[33]

Processed foods

A highly consolidated distribution process encourages large supermarket chains to feature industrial food products instead of more diverse foods produced by small-scale sustainable growers. Massive distributors deal almost exclusively with equally massive food producers, and pass along their lack of choice to the consumer. As a result, small-scale growers, which tend to produce a greater variety of crops and ingredients, must use other means of distributing their products; farmers markets, community-supported agriculture and organic retail outlets to get their products into the hands of consumers.[34]

Processed food has been one of the main culprits accused of creating an obese nation. A Friends of the Earth survey[35] of Britain's leading supermarkets found that the majority of items being promoted were fatty and sugary processed foods. In the long term, a diet high in fatty, sugary and/or salty foods increases the risk of developing coronary heart disease, some cancers, hypertension, diabetes and numerous other health disorders.[36]

The cost of healthy eating

Eating healthy food can be expensive from supermarkets. In another Friends of the Earth survey, two baskets of food, one healthier, and the other less so, were priced in several supermarkets in a deprived inner London area and in a more affluent London suburb. The healthier basket cost more than the less healthy one in both areas, but the healthier basket cost was greatest in the supermarkets in the low-income areas.[37]

Poor diet and its related health problems cost the NHS at least £2 billion each year. Obesity has almost trebled in England since the early 1980s; 21 per cent of women and 19 per cent of men are now classified as obese with a further 33 per cent of women and 44 per cent of men classified as overweight. The costs of obesity across the economy as a whole could run to £2.5 billion a year.[38]

In more recent years, food consumption patterns have become more favourable. The consumption of fruit and vegetables has increased by 10 per cent over the last 10 years while the percentage of energy derived from fat has declined and now stands at 38.2 per cent (targets recommended in Dietary Reference Values are 35 per cent).[39] However, excessive salt consumption is still a health issue, contributing to high blood pressure, strokes, heart attacks and osteoporosis. In the UK, we consume around 12 grams of salt a day on average, a figure we are advised to cut to 6 grams.[40]

The UK government Department for Food and Rural Affairs (DEFRA) states that food-consumption patterns are being shaped by increasingly affluent and informed consumers. But current eating patterns, if continued, may also lead to a segmentation of society between the 'disciplined' (who take health into account) and the 'undisciplined' (who do not), leading to subsequent health and nutrition problems. For example, the death rate from coronary heart disease is three times higher amongst the unskilled than amongst professionals, and this gap has widened over the latest 20 years for which figures are available. These differences are mirrored in the patterns of food consumption; lower-income families find it more difficult to pay for expensive healthy foods. At the same time higher-income households consume far more fruit and vegetables, reflecting both higher spending power but also other household characteristics (eg more ready access).[41]

Poor labelling

A 'healthy eating' logo has been introduced by the UK government as one contribution to a healthy diet. The World Health Organization has recommended – and the government has widely promoted – a 'five-a-day' campaign. Eating at least five portions of fruit and vegetables per day can reduce overall deaths from chronic disease by up to 20 per cent[42] and help ward off heart disease and some cancers.[43] In the UK, we consume only about three portions a day, and one fifth of children eat no fruit at all. In 2003, Tesco and Sainsbury's failed to sign up to use a new Department of Health logo designed to boost people's consumption of fruit and vegetables, although Sainsbury's was preparing to use its own five-a-day logo from May 2003. Gill Fine, Sainsbury's head of nutrition, commented: 'If we are trying to make it easier for people to eat more fruit and vegetables, we need more flexibility, we need to make it enjoyable.' The company would be putting its logo on foods, which had 'controlled' amounts of added salt, sugar and fats. She insisted the company fully backed the drive to encourage people to eat five portions a day. Tesco said that it has 'had our own logo for a couple of years. It has been really popular with customers, who appreciate the guidance it gives them.' Asda, however, is among about 50 companies adopting the Government scheme: 'We want to support the Government in a co-ordinated response that maximises the impact and helps get the message across,' it said.[44]

These standards are all very well, but according to the International Institute for Environment and Development, the UK and Europe suffer an additional cost to the primary producer. For instance, meat products grown elsewhere in the world under a very different regulatory regime are imported onto the shelves of the food retailers, competing with home-grown produce. UK pig producers, for example, have been frustrated that the stall-and-tether ban imposed by government has not translated into a premium for their higher welfare product when compared to imports. Meat imports rose from 25 per cent in 1990 to 33 per cent in 2000, and the situation has worsened in the last year because of foot-and-mouth disease.[45]

Apple growers feel equally strongly about supermarkets requiring British farmers to comply with Assured Produce schemes but filling up shelves with non-assured fruit from New Zealand and elsewhere, in the middle of the UK season when apples abound. The International Institute for Environment and Development reports:[46]

> *The agriculture time bomb created by the government and the supermarkets has finally exploded. The government's role has been to force farmers into high costs (welfare, feed, traceability etc) with no mechanism to enforce the same standards on imports. Imports are, therefore, cheaper and replace home production. The supermarkets force high standards on the farmer and then base the price on how cheaply they can buy imports.*
>
> Fred Henley, Seaton Ross, York[47]

and:

> *There's frustration with the supermarkets .*
> *. . They're using farm assured logos, and*
> *that should protect our products, but*
> *consumers see these next to products that*
> *aren't farm assured, and just because the*
> *retailer is selling it, they assume that they*
> *all conform to the same standards. The*
> *retailers aren't playing fairly, though*
> *they're a great place to sell our products.*

William Goodwin, dairy farmer from West
Sussex[48]

Such was the frustration about supermarkets obliging farmers to join Assured Produce schemes, which impose additional costs and obligations without adding any commercial value, that the Federation of Small Businesses lodged a complaint of restrictive trade practice at the Office of Fair Trading in 2000.[49] While the schemes can be a good discipline for farmers, they do have a cost; growers must conform to new requirements, private standards and codes of practice without any contribution from retailers to the extra cost or risk.[50]

Advertising to children

According to Kath Dalmeny of the Food Commission, British children are eating less than half the recommended amount of fruit and vegetables and more salt than the maximum recommended for adults. Over 80 per cent of children are exceeding the recommended quantities of sugar and over 90 per cent are eating more than the recommended amounts of saturated fat. Many children were also deficient in micronutrients such as iron, zinc and several vitamins, which are crucial in maintaining their long-term health.[51]

Such dietary imbalance raises the risk of a number of serious health problems. Nearly one in five English children were classified as overweight in the 1998 Health Survey for England,[52] and childhood obesity has been described as 'epidemic'. The prevalence of excess weight among English primary school children doubled between 1984 and 1998. Diabetes type 2, once considered a disease of middle age and closely linked to obesity, is now being reported among British adolescents. Other problems continue. Despite fluoridation, more than half of 4- to 18-year olds suffer from dental decay due to sugar. Girls approaching puberty are laying the nutritional foundations for their pregnancies, which in turn will affect the immediate and long-term health of the child.

Children establish at an early age food preferences and dietary habits that will continue into adult life. There are many influences on children's diets, including knowledge of nutrition, price, cultural and peer pressure and individual or family needs and tastes. However, supermarkets wield a particularly strong arm: the range of foods available on our shelves, the information provided on food packaging and, of course, the relentless marketing or advertising of food products, either directly to children or to their peer group or family. Unhealthy offers are often aimed specifically at children. The Food Commission found that Sainsbury's and Tesco were offering money-off vouchers for lunch box products such as sweets, hot dogs, sweetened cereal, jelly, chocolate, crisps and soft drinks in late 1999 and found little had changed by 2000.[53]

Supermarkets concede openly that the main target markets for fast-food and soft-drinks products are children and teenagers. In a survey of 358 foods marketed to children in the UK, the Food Commission discovered that 77 per cent of the products contained high levels of sugar, salt, saturated fat or total fat as judged against government nutrition guidelines. The survey focused on food that was likely to form a large part of children's diets, excluding 'treat' foods such as confectionery, crisps, soft drinks and bag snack foods. A mere seven per cent of the food products surveyed were found to be low in fat, saturated fat, sugar and salt. In addition, many of the children's foods, especially those of poorer nutritional quality, deliberately used colourings and flavourings to boost their attractiveness. Foods with a poor nutritional profile (in other words, those that should be eaten most sparingly) were found to be the ones that had been made the most appealing to children through a range of promotional techniques; bright packaging, intensely coloured and flavoured ingredients, free gifts and link-ups with cartoon characters, pop stars, sporting heroes and popular children's films. Such techniques were rarely employed to promote healthier eating options.[54]

Children who eat a regular diet of foods specifically marketed with them in mind are highly likely to face future health problems. A Consumers' Association survey of food labelling in 2003 found:[55]

1. Some food products featuring health claims were high in sugar, fat and/or salt.

2. A number of products had misleading or confusing labels and limited nutrition labelling.

3. A number of products may give consumers the impression that they contain more of the main ingredient than they actually do; eg, Sainsbury's Blue Parrot Café Mild Chicken Curry with Rice contains only 14 per cent chicken.

4. Labelling rules require manufacturers to label sodium but many do not label salt content. This confuses consumers because government recommendations for target average intake refer to salt, not sodium, which is not the same.

5. A number of tinned products are higher in sugar and salt than the adult equivalents. More worryingly, some of these products market themselves as having one portion of the recommended daily allowance of fruit and vegetables. But criteria have yet to be agreed as to what extent foods that are high in salt, fat and/or sugar can count towards this. A

number of products are using images and cartoons aimed at children to encourage the consumption of products high in sugar, fat or salt.

The UK boasts the highest concentration of food advertising aimed at children within the EU. Almost all food advertisements aimed at children are for confectionery, sugary cereals, ready-prepared foods and fast-food outlets. Yet only 13 per cent of parents want advertising to children banned and, at the other end of the spectrum, only a similarly small proportion admit that they fall prey to 'pester power' – a child's influence in their buying decisions. In 2003, The Family Food Survey was commissioned by the Food Advertising Unit, the UK food advertising industry body, and questioned more than 1,500 parents through a parenting website Raisingkids.co.uk. It revealed that 63 per cent of parents thought TV advertising prompted their children to ask to buy a product and 84 per cent believed that it manipulated children. However, 86 per cent said it is parents' responsibility to explain to their children that they could not have everything they saw advertised.[56]

Supermarkets have also come under fire from The Parents Jury (an independent panel representing 2,000 parents set up by the Food Commission) regarding supermarkets deliberately placing sweets and snacks within children's reach at their checkouts. The Parents Jury has launched a campaign called 'Chuck Snacks Off the Checkout' to put pressure on retailers to rethink their policies.[57]

In an effort to put the consumer's mind at rest over the whole issue of healthy food, Britain's major food companies, supermarkets and caterers launched a coalition in 2003, specifically aimed at combating high rates of obesity in children.[58] However, campaigners see this merely as a belated attempt to fend off the imposition of much stricter regulations over food:

> *The food giants are so powerful and so arrogant that they have seen themselves as untouchable. I hope that they achieve something real, and that they don't come up with some token gesture of corporate responsibility, like a new label or low-fat product.*
>
> Professor Tim Lang, City University[59]

The verdict

We should all care about the food we eat; what it is made of, where it comes from, how it tastes. Supermarkets sell us the image of clean, cheap and healthy food but the reality is very different. We are quickly becoming a nation unable to identify fruit or vegetables, cook them or provide a healthy diet to our children or ourselves. Consumers need to gain control over their food before it is too late, and the following advice may help:

20 ways to change the food system[60]

1. Buy from your local independent shops; including grocers, butchers, bakers, newsagents, and pharmacies whenever you can. Smile at the shopkeeper!

2. Read the labels on your food. If you do not recognise the ingredients, put the product back on the shelf. As a useful rule of thumb, the more heavily processed a food, the poorer the nutrition is likely to be.

3. Buy fish and seafood certified with the blue Marine Stewardship Council logo, which means that it comes from a sustainable, well-managed fishery.

4. Put a chart of what's in season in this country on your fridge. Buy seasonal, locally produced food whenever you can. Stop routinely buying food that is out of season.

5. Join a box-delivery scheme or a food co-op. Buy organic if you can. Shopping this way ensures more of the profits go back to the producers.

6. Look out for food miles and choose produce that clocks up the fewest.

7. Make the effort to scrutinise local planning applications, particularly if they involve changes in shops and supermarkets.

8. Say no to plastic bags. Where there is a choice, go for produce that uses the least packaging.

9. Write to the Independent Television Commission demanding tougher controls on food advertising on TV aimed at children.

10. Pressure your local council, school governors, hospital trusts and your employer to buy local, seasonal and organic food when awarding catering contracts for their canteens. Write to your MP demanding a change in the way public institutions buy their food.

11. Buy fair trade products whenever you can.

12. Be brave and ask about what's going into your takeaway. Has the chicken been injected with water, is the chip oil fresh?

13. Cook a meal with a child.

14. Help your school implement a healthy-eating policy. Refuse to allow private companies to market to your children through school.

15. Do your bit to break up the concentration of corporate power in the food industry. Write to your MEP asking them to push for the code of conduct regulating European transnational corporations (TNCs) operating in developing countries, which aims to make big business more accountable.

16. Write to your MP asking her or him to lobby for competition policy to be changed to take account of public interest, as in France.

17. Support organisations pressuring government and supermarkets for change, such as Oxfam, the Food Commission, Friends of the Earth, the Consumers' Association, or Sustain. Send them money if you can.

18. Slow down. Wash your own salad, and improve the quality of your life.

19. Remember the power of the boycott.

20. Use good-food directories.

Chapter 6

Employees and Workers

They have cut hours, they are asking you to take holidays unpaid, working conditions are quite poor, you get no respect or thank you, managers change quite regularly. Morale is really low. You have not got the pay rises compared to other companies. They could pay a lot better for the jobs we are doing. There are not many full-timers; there are an awful lot of part-timers. I was doing full-time hours but my contract was only 28 [hours]. But if I was ever off sick or [on] holiday, you got your basic hours [28 hours]. I can't see it getting any worse – its got to get better. They have to buck their ideas up and look after the staff more because everyone feels absolutely fed up. Just a better place to work in. The pay is not really an issue; just a bit more respect.

Sainsbury's employee for 15 years,
January 2004

This is one of my real hates of the organisation [Asda]. It boils down to two things. One is what it looks like to the public: so we are all co-workers – 'the stars are in the stores', that's what they used to say. And yet when it came down to giving bonuses, the difference was huge. Store staff get £250 – if they are lucky – bonus. The same in distribution centres. Head office staff, the lowest they got is 10% of their salary and the most they got was 100%. Most people at head office were on 35% bonus. They [store staff] were looked down on by head office – there's no two-ways about it. A good example [that] is they push this flexible working idea. If you have got children you are allowed to do the school run. And yet when it comes down to it, when I asked if I could come in late one day a week and make it up, I was told absolutely no way – what would the business look like if everyone came in at ten o'clock. It's absolutely shocking, but you read in the paper, you read about belief leave and grandparents' day and [a]whole range of things they will do for their employees. Reality is that it didn't happen.

Ex Asda Manager, January 2004

This chapter looks at the impact on supermarket workers as both a direct and indirect result of supermarket policy and practice. The food and retailing industries are notorious for having some of the worst working conditions in the country. Combine these industries and you get supermarkets. With the drive for low-cost food, the easiest target is their own employees' wages and conditions. This means part-time employees, mostly women: some of whom are not earning enough to pay National Insurance or are illegal immigrants.

Employees not working directly for the multiples suffer too; in 2003, supermarkets were accused by the UK Parliament of encouraging 'gangmaster' labour on farms where illegal immigrants are used and employment law is ignored. This isn't limited to the UK; a consequence of globalised supply chains is that cheap labour – and with it child labour, slaves, poverty wages and dangerous working conditions – in developing countries is used for the production of our food. Some supermarkets have responded by implementing codes of conduct but these often only cover basic human and workers' rights. This chapter looks at those at the top of the supermarket power triangle; executives who, while often exploiting the vulnerable, take pains to reward themselves with 'fat cat' salaries above and beyond any what is morally and financially reasonable.

Working conditions for supermarket employees

Supermarket supply chains are like tentacles with a huge number of suppliers and sub-contractors extending in all directions and all over the world. Supermarket employees are a major element in the UK workforce, with the 10 largest players employing around 700,000 workers, compared to 300,000 in food manufacturing and 120,000 permanent farm employees[1] (see table below).

Number of retail staff employed by major supermarkets[2]	
Tesco	171,737 (includes section managers)
Sainsbury's	110,000
Somerfield	39,000
Morrisons	33,000
Marks and Spencer	53,500 (includes managers)

It is not only the consumer who suffers from a reduction of choice and power, as we've already seen; employees working for large supermarkets are also worse off. Supermarkets employ large numbers of unskilled women, students, school children and disabled workers, often paying them on starter rates so that, with the high staff turnover that is characteristic in the industry, labour costs are kept to a minimum, with this group rarely climbing further up the ladder before moving elsewhere.[3]

In 2003, police in the US arrested and deported 300 hundred illegal immigrants working for Wal-Mart. The cleaning staff (working for subcontractors) stated that they had been forced to work seven nights a week without overtime benefits or workers' compensation coverage in the case of injury or health problems. Wal-Mart has been widely reported to have told new employees how to apply for food stamps so that they could reach the end of each month without starving. The superstore claimed in its defence it was not responsible for the illegal workers, as subcontractors hired and fired cleaning staff. US federal prosecutors disagree and pointed out that police had previously raided Wal-Mart stores, arresting illegal immigrants in 1998 and 2001.[4]

More supermarkets mean fewer and worse paid jobs, which is ultimately bad for both the local and national economy. There are no specific regulations to protect supermarket employees. Although most of the major supermarkets recognise unions, the arrival of Wal-Mart and an American work ethic brings with it unethical threats of its own. There has been a constant stream of accusations levied at Wal-Mart concerning its anti-union stance and use of 'sweatshop' conditions in the Third World factories that supply some of its goods.[5]

Despite Wal-Mart's denial of these claims, since Asda's merger with this American giant, the GMB union ('Britain's General Union', who represents staff in supermarkets and their suppliers) has seen its position threatened by the supermarket's reluctance to publicise its existence amongst new recruits. The position of unions in other supermarkets is already precarious and it seems likely that, as is the case with all supermarket practices – from loyalty schemes to loss-leading pricing strategies – others will follow where one leads. Homogeneity is the key to survival and Wal-Mart leads the way.[6]

According to the United Food and Commercial Workers international union (UFCW), Wal-Mart has fallen foul of labour watchdogs on a number of counts, including:[7]

- **Paying low wages that often preclude employees taking out health insurance.**

- **Preventing employees from joining unions.**

- **Imposing lax safety and compensation standards.**

- **Employing predatory pricing tactics to close down small local competitors.**

Campaigners say that a particular concern is that the company – whose last annual sales were worth US $200 billion – is now beginning to export its practices overseas by demanding that suppliers elsewhere similarly reduce wages and benefits in order to cut costs.[8]

According to Julie Smith in a report entitled 'Race to the Top' for the International Institute for Environment and Development, a supermarket's drive to lower input costs and increase the amount and variety of food can result in high social costs for the workers involved.[9] The growing retail sector has created thousands of low-paid, often part-time jobs. Over two thirds of employees in food retailing are part-time and the majority are women, with a large number of students and temporary or agency workers included. Sainsbury's, for example, increased part-time employees from 45,000 in 1989 to 84,500 in 1998. In total, 69 per cent of all staff worked part-time and 75 per cent were women.[10]

UK government legislation and European regulations have provided an improved framework of minimum labour standards for supermarket employees, which includes trade union recognition, the national minimum wage and regulations that prohibit discrimination against part-time workers.[11]

But what are the realities? The proposed EU directive to provide temporary agency workers with equal pay and conditions after six weeks' employment ran into trouble and was blocked by the UK government. The UK has until March 2005 to implement a EU directive establishing a general framework for informing and consulting employees.[12]

The national minimum wage (NMW) has undoubtedly improved pay for those on the bottom tier of the pay structure. Despite this, retail cash-desk and checkout operators (84 per cent of whom are women) fall in the bottom 10 percent of non-manual occupations with average full-time earnings of only £184.70 per week. In addition, the latest New Earnings Survey concluded that part-time women earned just 58.6 per cent of the hourly rate of full-time male workers. Many of the multiples have recently moved their lowest rates above the NMW of £4.20 (implemented in October 2002) to be more competitive; Tesco pays an hourly rate of £5.16 for those over 18, Sainsbury's £4.81 and Safeway £4.62.[13] Some supermarket chains have also reviewed their youth and adult rates. It is common practice for the supermarkets to pay at least the NMW for staff at age 18 (the statutory age is 22) and the rates paid to staff aged 16 and 17 tend to be above the established rate of £3.60. For example, the Co-op sets a minimum rate of £4.28 for newly appointed staff aged 18 or over at national level; although the company allows some local variation in order to recruit and retain staff.[14]

Another variable affecting pay rates includes length of service. Many employees start on lower rates that are increased after an initial period of training. For example, Safeway checkout operators' pay increases from £4.50 to £4.72 after a 3-month induction programme and Sainsbury's 2002 rates rose from £4.21 to £4.47 after a similar period of time. Similarly, there are regional variations; Marks and Spencer include three levels of London allowance paid on top of basic rates and Tesco brought in new, zonal pay bands in August 2000. Both the Co-op and Sainsbury's also operate a number of higher pay zones to accommodate varying pay pressures in different parts of the country.[15]

Flexible hours are also another important issue. While parents with children under 6 or of disabled children under 18 are able to request flexible working hours under new family-friendly employment rights (and most supermarket retail employees already work flexible hours), staff can find their hours altered arbitrarily by managers to cover busy periods or staff shortages. Similarly, some of these staff are employed on short-hours contracts to specifically cover extended opening hours, which include Sundays. Furthermore, workers' rights, for example being able to decline to work on Sundays, have been eroded in many cases. However, Sunday premium payments, which tended to be double-time, or a day off in lieu, are being phased out by some supermarkets as Sunday is now generally accepted as part of the working week in the retail sector.[16]

While benefit packages such as pensions make an important contribution to the job for those who qualify, many do not. In 1998, 40 per cent of all employees did not earn enough to pay National Insurance contributions and were excluded from pensions and other contribution-based benefits.[17] According to Julie Smith, benefit packages make an important contribution to the job for those who qualify. Many do not. The TUC reported that:[18]

> *With many working women currently earning too little to pay into pension schemes, the TUC is concerned that another . . . generation of poor female pensioners is being created. Recent figures from the Equal Opportunities Commission suggest that only four in ten (37 per cent of) women who work part time have access to any kind of pension scheme, yet nearly half (44 per cent) of all female employees are part timers.'*

The long-term financial security of these workers when they get to retirement age is bleak, and supermarkets need to address this issue.

' Gangmaster' labour

The issue of 'gangmaster' labour on farms – where casual labour for crop picking and packing are often supplied by small, informal employment businesses – is another issue of concern. Many 'gangmasters' operate in breach of agricultural wages orders as well as breaking rules about payment of income tax and NI contributions; trade union recognition is either low or non-existent.[19] The Environment, Food and Rural Affairs Select

Committee published a report on gangmasters in 2003. The report highlights that a significant number of gang-masters are involved in illegal activity including:[20]

- **The non-payment of taxes.**

- **The employment of illegal workers from abroad, who are often housed in appalling conditions.**

- **The flouting of employment legislation.**

It not only criticised the government for failing to provide sufficient resources and political leadership to confront the complex problems in the industry but also concluded that:

> *The dominant position of the supermarkets in relation to their suppliers is a significant contributory factor in creating an environment where illegal activity by gangmasters can take root.*[21]

The Committee called on the major supermarkets to re-examine their policies on the labour used by their suppliers and called on the UK government Department of Trade and Industry to re-examine the relationship between supermarkets and their suppliers.[22]

Workers in developing countries

It is now supermarket policy to offer year-round supplies of fresh-produce lines, requiring sourcing from different areas around the world. In 1990, it was estimated that trade in fresh fruit, vegetables and cut flowers was equivalent to 5 per cent of global commodity trade; roughly equivalent to that of crude petroleum. Horticultural exports from the developing world have become a major sector in international trade. By the mid 1990s, developing countries contributed a third by value to this trade, twice the value of their traditional agricultural exports. Five countries – Argentina, Brazil, China, Kenya and Mexico – account for over 40 per cent of world trade in these highly perishable items from developing countries. An increasing number of African countries, such as the Ivory Coast, Kenya, South Africa and Zimbabwe, have entered this trade. The competitiveness of African suppliers on high-value horticultural produce depends on their low costs of production, relatively short flight times and ability to supply produce of the quality and quantity required by international markets. Cut flower, vegetable and fruit producers in Kenya 'proudly claim that, within 48 hours of being harvested, produce can be on the UK supermarket shelf.'[23]

However, workers from all over the world are working in poor conditions, for low wages and with little or no protection from exploitation to produce these goods. Currently, 1.3 billion people work in agriculture-related jobs. A full half of the world's labour force, 450 million people, are waged agricultural workers. Questions are increasingly being asked about the fairness of trade between consumers and the workers along the food chain. The rights of these workers, like the rights of workers in the UK, have become an issue that concerns retailers, unions, consumers and shareholders of supermarket companies. The globalised structure of agribusiness has increased the vulnerability of those working in the food industry, and the irony is that those who feed the world are often least able to feed themselves.[24]

Some supermarkets in the UK operate ethical trading or codes of conduct for sourcing products, to help producers, suppliers and the managers of their own operations to operate above 'accepted' minimum limits. These codes often include decent minimum wage levels, health and safety issues, employee rights and working practices. Consumers can buy from businesses operating ethical trade schemes safe in the knowledge that the product has not been made through the exploitation of employees in developing countries. At the moment, ethical trade is a relatively new concept and is still being developed, and there are only a few product lines in supermarkets that are conforming to an ethical code of conduct. These vary, but can include the vegetables and flowers grown in West Africa mentioned earlier. Many companies are aware of the issues but seem less than enthusiastic or confident about making any great changes until consumers buy sufficiently large numbers of ethical trade products.[25]

According to William Young and Richard Welford in *Ethical Shopping – Where to Shop, What to Buy and What to Do to Make a Difference,* supermarkets can certainly get help with moving towards sound sourcing and the development of codes of conduct. There are many industry initiatives beginning to spring up that supermarkets or manufacturers can join. Some companies have adopted the UK Ethical Trading Initiative (ETI) 'Base Code', which is voluntary (see below). For example, Sainsbury's is a founding member of the ETI and Safeway, Asda, Co-op, Marks and Spencer, Somerfield and Tesco are all members. Going further, companies can choose to be certified (independently inspected for compliance) to the US Social Accountability Standard (SA8000) or the UN Global Compact. The latter is a voluntary charter that companies can sign up for to protect the environment, labour and human rights.[26]

The scope for increased ethical trade is enormous; most UK supermarkets could and should get involved in ethical trade. And we as consumers can help to encourage companies to do more by making our purchases count and by asking questions about codes of conduct when we are considering making purchases of goods sourced in developing countries.[27]

Ethical Trading Initiative (ETI)[28]

The Ethical Trading Initiative's role is to identify and promote good practice in the implementation of codes of labour practice, including the monitoring and independent verification of the observance of code provisions by companies. It is an alliance of companies, non-governmental organisations (NGOs), and trade union organisations committed to working together to fulfil this role.

ETI member companies are committed to adopting codes based on internationally agreed standards, and moving to the demonstrable implementation of their codes. ETI is a learning organisation rather than a certification body. The ETI Base Code (which is voluntary and not certified by the ETI) contains the following provisions:

- Measures against forced labour.

- Freedom of association and the right to collective bargaining.

- Safe and hygienic working conditions.

- No child labour to be used.

- Living wages to be paid.

- No excessive working hours.

- No discrimination.

- Regular employment to be provided.

- No harsh or inhumane treatment.

These provisions reflect the relevant declarations and conventions of the United Nations and the International Labour Organisation (ILO), including the core conventions of the ILO and its 1998 Geneva Declaration on Fundamental Principles and Rights at Work.

Website: www.ethicaltrade.org

In countries where national labour laws operate effectively and trade unions are recognised and have collective bargaining rights, codes are an additional support. In countries without these laws, codes are often the only means for workers to secure basic human rights. Implementation of pay and benefit packages for UK retail staff by the supermarkets is a complex but open process; addressing labour standards issues for all their worldwide suppliers and sub-contractors is more complex, and this is new territory.[29]

Sainsbury's:

> *has policies covering all aspects of ethical trade, and personnel responsible for managing and co-ordinating the work being carried out by ourselves and our suppliers. Our socially responsible sourcing initiative focuses on looking at the welfare and labour conditions of workers within the supply chain of own-brand products to Sainsbury's.*[30]

Sainsbury's initially established a code of practice on socially responsible sourcing in early 1998, and this has been issued to all the company's own, brand suppliers. It now has a programme of visiting suppliers to monitor issues associated with the Code, carried out as part of the normal monitoring and inspection process. Suppliers are expected to take responsibility for sub-contractors. Sainsbury's has also evaluated a number of external social auditing companies in order to understand how they operate and the advantages of working with them.[31]

The Co-operative Group has been a leader in social accountability and adopted its own Code of Business Conduct in March 1997 and revised it in February 2001. It articulates the values and standards the Society expects to apply in the course of conducting its business. These include self-help, self-responsibility, democracy, equality, equity, solidarity, honesty, openness, social responsibility and caring for others. Every employee is given a copy of the Code and it also forms part of the terms of employment. Breaches may lead to disciplinary action, including dismissal. The Co-op is now developing a core set of social performance indicators for all of its activities. The indicators will address social responsiveness; customer service; environmental performance; community involvement; employee conditions and training; workforce diversity; applying values in supply chain; and the affinity members demonstrate to the values.[32]

However, these policies comply to minimum standards and do not help smaller overseas producers of export crops such as coffee and cocoa, which are in crisis. Coffee, for instance, has a surplus in world supply (in part due to changes in market structure rather than larger stocks), and farm prices have collapsed, falling below cost of production for many of the world's 20–30 million farmers who depend on the coffee harvest. 70 per cent of these farmers are smallholders. But these low prices paid to some of the world's poorest and most powerless citizens are not reflected on the supermarket shelves.[33]

Here 'fair trade' is the answer, offering a practical way of helping producers establish themselves into the worldwide supply chain. Fair trade was introduced to ensure a better deal for farmers, growers and small-scale producers, who in the past have often found that, because of their remoteness or size of operation, they were unable to obtain a fair price for their products. Fair trade targets these disadvantaged communities to enable them to be involved in international trade. Building up the skills and capacity of producer groups is central, enabling them to trade more effectively with fair-trade organisations and, for some, to begin to export to mainstream buyers in developed economies.[34]

Even more importantly, fair-trade companies often provide pre-payment so that crops can be purchased without producers getting into insupportable debt, as well as paying a guaranteed minimum price above the marketplace norm. They also include an additional 'social premium', so that farmers and growers can invest in their businesses without going into debt, and support local social welfare programmes such as education and health initiatives. The local community decides democratically how to invest their extra income, ensuring that participation and joint responsibility are of key importance. Providing access to information about global markets is an important feature of fair trade.[35]

There are over 1,000 fair-trade labelled products in 17 countries, with sales of £120 million in Europe. In the UK, sales of FAIRTRADE Mark products have increased by about 53 per cent per year over the last 5 years. The information below describes the FAIRTRADE Mark scheme, which consumers can identify as a label of assurance.[36]

The FAIRTRADE Mark scheme[37]

The Fairtrade Foundation awards an independent consumer guarantee – the FAIRTRADE Mark (see next page) – to individual products, that meet Fairtrade criteria regarding terms of trade and conditions of production.

The main points of meeting the FAIRTRADE Mark criteria are:

1. Production conditions:

- Small-scale farmers who produce the product can participate in a democratic organisation.

- Plantation/factory workers can participate in trade union activities and have decent wages, housing, and health and safety standards.

- No child or forced labour.

- Programmes for environmental sustainability.

2. Fairtrade terms of trading:

- A price that covers the cost of production.

- A social 'premium' to be used by the producers to improve their living and working conditions.

- Advance payment to avoid small producer organisations falling into debt.

- Contracts that allow long-term planning and sustainable production practices.

Some FAIRTRADE Mark companies and their products include:

- Cafedirect (instant and ground coffee, and tea).

- Clipper Teas (teabags and loose-leaf teas).

- Co-op (bananas, coffee and own-label chocolates).

- The Day Chocolate Company (Divine Chocolate products, Dubble Milk Chocolate Crispy Crunch Bar).

- Equal Exchange (teas, coffees, honey, sugar, cocoa).

- Green & Black's (chocolate and cocoa).

- The Hampstead Tea & Coffee Co (speciality teas).

- Oxfam (chocolate and cocoa).

- Ridgeways (tea bags and loose tea).

- Traidcraft (chocolate, cookies and snack bars).

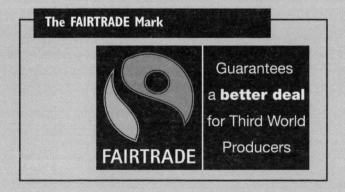

The FAIRTRADE Mark

FAIRTRADE

Guarantees a **better deal** for Third World Producers

Supermarkets stock products with the FAIRTRADE Mark to varying degrees. Some have even made their own-label products certified to the FAIRTRADE Mark; the Co-operative Group, for example, has switched all own-brand coffee to fair-trade sources in 2003. This is a great breakthrough for the fair-trade movement in terms of mainstreaming its products. The only worry is that pioneers of fair-trade products, such as Traidcraft and The Day Chocolate Company, provide initiatives that go well beyond the FAIRTRADE Mark rules. Supermarkets own-label products may not provide these extra initiatives in the producer communities and only conform strictly to the FAIRTRADE Mark rules. And the FAIRTRADE Mark only covers a limited range of products, while supermarkets offer an ever-increasing range of products and services.

Another route to fair trade is via organisations creating their own initiatives and working with others. Organisations such as Oxfam, Traidcraft and The Body Shop International have developed a reputation for selling fair-trade products using their own criteria. These organisations might have some products with the FAIRTRADE Mark, but in general apply fair-trade principles to most of their products and practices, as well as participating in developmental, political and charitable activities. These organisations have expanded the fair-trade principles into handicrafts, clothes and beauty products as well as food products.[38] Supermarkets could do the same to expand the impact of fair-trade products.

Fat cat salaries

In 2003, it was reported by the *Guardian* newspaper that Marks and Spencer is paying for its chairman, Luc Vandevelde, to live at London's luxurious Claridge's hotel in Mayfair as part of a pay package worth nearly £1 million a year for a three-day-a-week job. Under the terms of a contract that is far more generous than usual for a non-executive chairman, Vandevelde gets a basic salary of £420,000, with the opportunity of doubling it if he meets performance targets. The Belgian businessman also receives a pension benefit of £67,000 and a car allowance of £18,000. In an extraordinary clause that surprised shareholders, M&S agreed to put him up at Claridges' for the three days a week when he is working for the company. Situated in the heart of Mayfair, Claridge's suites begin at £675 a night, with top-drawer penthouses commanding a nightly rate of £3,500.[39]

Seven senior directors of Marks and Spencer shared more than £2.4 million in bonuses last year compared with the average annual bonus of £624 received by the 65,000 staff. Chairman Luc Vandevelde picked up £617,000 to take his total pay over £1.7 million, while his chief executive Roger Holmes was granted £491,000. The supermarket also paid Alan McWalter £451,000 for loss of office after he left as marketing director in July last year. He received a package of £666,000 for four months' work.[40]

Meanwhile, at Tesco the executive directors will receive a minimum of five years' salary under 'termination provisions' revealed for the first time this year under a complex 'executive incentive scheme'. This suggests that Sir Terry Leahy, chief executive, will receive five times his basic £916,000 salary; around £4.6 million, on top of entitlements under his two-year contract. With bonuses and incentive schemes, Sir Terry was paid £2.8 million in 2002.[41] Sainsbury's under-fire chief executive Sir Peter Davis has negotiated a new award of shares for himself currently worth £4 million for agreeing to move up to the chairman's office in 2004. He will receive the full payout even if he misses profit targets by 10 per cent; if he misses by 30 per cent he will still get half the shares promised even if he is fired.[42]

The verdict

Supermarkets, consumers and society generally need to have a serious look at the issues raised here. The contrast in income between the top and bottom within the supermarket pyramid as well as with their suppliers is stark; it is often highlighted as the consequence of globalisation. The National Minimum Wage and ethical trading codes of conduct only provide a minimum for workers to survive. The tendency for supermarkets appears to be to use these as their standards and not (as they should be regarded) a minimum safety net: this results in their dragging down overall wages and the level of human or workers' rights. Supermarkets need to recognise this as an issue and move towards improving the conditions of their own employees and suppliers. This is even more important as supermarkets are expanding their range of products from groceries to clothes, shoes and toys, areas where human rights abuses in suppliers in developing countries are well documented.

Chapter 7

Supermarkets' Abuse
of Power

One of the key issues discussed in this book is the power that supermarkets have over the grocery market and consequently over consumers, suppliers, communities, the food we eat, employees and the environment. Supermarkets use this power to kill off competitors, whether they are greengrocers or chemists, and force suppliers and farmers to accept low prices for their products and to shoulder all the risk of the ebb and flow of consumer demand. Consumers are lured into supermarkets with offers of cheap bread and milk, only to return home with large food bills and not very much to show for it.

Government policy has not helped this power by appointing supermarket representatives in key government committees and discouraging competition between supermarkets and independent retailers. This favours the domination of supermarkets. The government's Competition Commission has twice examined the concerns over supermarket power but has only reinforced their domination. The appalling amount of power wielded by the biggest supermarket in the world – Wal-Mart in the US – is a shocking example of what the future may hold for the UK.

Pricing out competitors

'It's so much cheaper at a supermarket.' But is it really? Not necessarily; the Competition Commission found in 2000 that supermarkets were putting prices up in areas where there was no strong competition. Supermarkets have also been in trouble with the Advertising Standards Authority (ASA) on numerous occasions for misleading advertisements and, in October 2001, Tesco was found guilty of putting up the price of goods just before a new £100 million, heavily publicised price-cutting campaign, in order to make the cuts seem more dramatic.[1]

Although general food prices have increased by less than average of all retails prices on the UK high street, the price of healthy foods has increased by more than average. Supermarkets are doing little to help matters. Key items such as bread and milk are certainly cheaper in supermarkets, because they are used as 'loss leaders' to entice customers into the store.[2] These are referred to as 'Known Value Items', where consumers are more likely to know the price of a product and compare it to other shops.

But not all products are so cheap. A simple comparison of fresh produce shows you can often get it cheaper at a local independent store. Exposing the myth that supermarkets are cheap, a survey for Sustain in 2000 found that fruit and vegetables were around 30 per cent cheaper at market stalls than supermarkets.[3] Similarly, a Friends of the Earth survey of apple pricing, showed that on average, a kilo of non-organic Cox apples cost 43p more in a supermarket than on a market stall (ie £1.45 at a supermarket, £1.07 at a greengrocer and £1.02 on a market stall). Bramley apples cost per kilo £1.22 at a supermarket, £1.02 at a greengrocer and 99p on a market stall; greengrocers were shown to be cheaper than supermarkets in most cases.[4]

The Competition Commission, which scrutinised supermarket competition in 2000 and again during the Safeway merger inquiry in 2003, has ironically reinforced supermarkets' power over groceries and other markets. The focus of the Commission has been only between large supermarkets; ie the more the better for competition. This is based on the premise of 'one-stop shopping' (going once a month or week to a supermarket and buying all the food you need for that period) versus 'secondary shopping' (shopping for additional items to supplement the monthly/weekly shop) and 'convenience shopping' (shopping for daily items). The Commission has ruled that there should be no less than five competing supermarkets in a local area, to encourage a 'competitive' environment for the large supermarkets. However, this only saturates the market with major supermarket chains, providing no opportunity for local competition in the form of local specialist shops (butchers, chemists and bakers or local, smaller supermarkets). It may well be the case that the majority of shopping takes place in the large supermarkets, but the Competition Commission inquiries have simply assisted the few large companies to dominate the market and have not provided an opportunity within the market for local shops. What is needed is real competition, where consumers have a choice other than the big four supermarkets.

However, one amber light given to the supermarkets was that the Commons Health Committee, in 2003, came out against the planned deregulation of pharmacy licences, where only a certain number of pharmacies are able to operate in a region. It saw that deregulation and the expansion of supermarket pharmacies could lead to the closure of existing independent pharmacies, threatening rural and deprived areas, and the oldest and poorest of our population.[5] Direct competition between independent pharmacies and supermarkets would lead to supermarkets using their buying power and 'one-stop shop' advantage to dominate the market. This would lead, as has been seen for other independents, to the closure of local pharmacies, killing off real choice and competition.

Exploiting consumers

We have already looked at how the multiples exert their buying power over suppliers: especially those supplying fresh produce, meat products, dairy and bakery products, forcing them to participate in promotions of a particular line, selling at a lower price and even result at a loss.[6] Another area supermarkets exploit for easy profit is in the 'added value' sector; adding perceived value to a product without necessarily changing the taste.

The scope for differentiating and processing even simple items is shown below; the price charged for Class 1 (the best) carrots in one supermarket in the Brighton area was 39.4p per kilo for loose carrots. Putting the same carrots into bags doubled the price. The price of peeled and sliced carrots was seven times as high as the loose product, at £2.83p per kilo, while a new product variety, the 'mini-crunch' carrot designed as a snack, retailed for £6.00 per kilo. Clearly, this adds significantly to supermarket margins.[7]

Adding value to carrots [8]		
Product	**Weight and price**	**Price per kilo**
Basic carrots, (Class I)	loose, 18p per lb.	39.40p
Basic carrots, bagged (Class I)	I kg bag, 87p	0.87p
Peeled and sliced carrots, bagged	350g bag, 99p	£2.83p
Carrot batons (peeled, chopped, washed, ready-to-eat)	200g bag, 59p	£2.95p
Peeled, ready-to-cook mini-carrots	300g bag, 85p	£2.83
Mini-carrots, in tray	225g tray, 99p	£4.40
Mini-crunch carrots (peeled, chopped, washed, ready-to-eat)	100g bag, 60p	£6.00

It is often hard for the consumer to compare prices quickly as different combinations of price-per-weight measures are often used on labels (ie pounds or pence per kilo, quarter kilo, gram or imperial pounds). The pull is the appearance and convenience to the consumer of the value-added food, leading to the shopping bill being often significantly higher than anticipated.

Influencing government

The major supermarkets enjoy enormous political influence in Britain. David Sainsbury, the chain's former chief executive and one of the richest men in the UK, is Minister for Science and Innovation and a major donor to the Labour Party. Tesco executives sit on six government task forces and made a £12 million donation to the Millennium Dome.[9] When supermarkets are negotiating planning approval with local councils for a new superstore, it is not unusual for them to add community facilities into their plans in exchange for planning consent. These kinds of agreements are called 'planning gain' – to allow a local community to benefit when land is sold for development[10] – and they are perfectly legal. George Monbiot, author of *Captive State – The Corporate Takeover of Britain*, cites some examples of Tesco negotiating planning deals:[11]

1. **In Kent, it offered to give £200,000 to the local authority's park-and-ride scheme and pay £300,000 for a community centre if it received planning permission for a new store.**

2. **In Oxfordshire, it announced that it would pay £6.6 million for a new road if its application were successful.**

3. In Bristol, it received permission to build a new store on a Greenfield site on the condition that it paid for an all-weather football pitch.

Takeover fever

In 2003, Morrisons, Sainsbury's, Tesco and Asda, along with some others, fought over the acquisition of Safeway through the Competition Commission. The Consumers' Association threw its support behind Morrisons, arguing that a 'fourth aggressive player in the market would strengthen consumer choice and ensure consumers have as competitive a market as possible.'[12] A letter to the Trade and Industry Secretary Patricia Hewitt about the bids for Safeway, by a group led by Friends of the Earth (and including the Institute of Asian Businesses, The National Federation of Women's Institutes, the British Independent Fruit Growers Association and the National Consumer Federation) highlighted their concerns. These included:[13]

- The ability of smaller supermarket chains, independent retailers and community pharmacies to compete at local, regional and national levels; and the related impacts on local economies.

- The impact on suppliers, particularly small businesses and farmers, due to increased buying power.

- The effect on consumer choice directly due to removal of one company from the market, and indirectly due to increased buyer power resulting from the takeover, which may result in loss of smaller retailers and in reduced innovation by suppliers.

- The impact on access to a healthy diet, eg through price wars targeting the least wholesome products, further erosion of local suppliers in urban and rural communities, and reduction of outlets accessible without a car.

The National Consumer Council had similar concerns:[14]

- Protecting the interests of people living in deprived areas, whether rural or urban, so they are not disadvantaged by the proposed acquisitions of Safeway.

- The risk of further reducing shoppers' choice by creating local monopolies.

- The impact of increasing the market power of the three main players at a national level, and difficulties faced by small competitors trying to enter the market.

In the summer of 2003, during Safeway 'takeover fever', Sainsbury's (while still being part of the Competition

Commission's inquiry regarding its bid for Safeway), was referred to the Competition Commission for its potential bid for Somerfield.[15] Soon after, Sainsbury's withdrew its intentions, with Sir Peter Davis, Sainsbury's chief executive, complaining:

> *I was disappointed with the outcome of the regulatory process. However, given the current level of regulatory uncertainty in the food retail sector, we have decided not to pursue the transaction any further.*[16]

Takeover fever is not a British disease. In response to Wal-Mart's acquisitions in the European market, the pan-European grocery titans are reshaping the retail landscape. The mega-merger of French corporations Carrefour and Promodès in 1999 created a clear market leader, operating in France, Italy, Spain, Portugal, Belgium and Greece. Some way behind is Tesco, which has made acquisitions in Ireland, Poland and the Far East. Both Carrefour and Dutch supermarket chain Royal Ahold (which already have stores in over twenty countries) have expressed an interest in entering the UK grocery sector. It is also likely that Wal-Mart will seek further mergers across Europe. Wal-Mart, with global sales of US $206.8 billion, is by far the world's biggest retailer; in 2002, its profits exceeded Exxon Mobil, enabling it to become the biggest company in the world.[17]

More mergers means larger multiples. To recap, Friends of the Earth details below how supermarkets, as a result of their sheer size and power, can be detrimental to consumers, farmers and small businesses:[18]

- Supermarkets do not offer the best price to consumers. Supermarket low prices are only on a very limited range of goods.

- Supermarkets favour imports over British produce. Although 84 per cent of shoppers say they want supermarkets to give preference to British produce when it is in season, the supermarkets appear to do the opposite.

- Supermarkets' bullying tactics can put small farmers out of business. For example, supermarkets pay invoices very late, and they pass costs back to suppliers for changes to transport and packaging and even for their own mistakes in ordering.

- Supermarkets are squeezing farmers' prices; for example, Tesco, which has the biggest market share, pays the lowest prices to farmers.

- Supermarkets are forcing small shops out of business. About eight independent shops close every day. Small independent shops cannot compete with the big multiples.

- Supermarkets do not support the local economy because local shops keep more money circulating in the region.

- Every time a large supermarket opens, on average 276 jobs are lost.

- Supermarkets import food over huge distances, resulting in large emissions of carbon dioxide.

- Supermarkets also transport food large distances around the UK due to their distribution system.

- Supermarkets waste food by placing difficult conditions on farmers for cosmetic appearance, often rejecting fresh produce though it is perfectly edible.

Wal-Mart's world domination

Andy Rowell in his article in the *Ecologist* quotes from Al Norman's book *Slam Dunking Wal-Mart – How You Can Stop Superstore Sprawl in Your Hometown*:

> *For saving a few cents, we are supposed to sacrifice 20 to 30 acres of land, lose jobs in other stores, and support low wage labour. It is a quality of life issue. You're surrounded by gridlock, and the architectural graffiti of a*

*windowless Wal-Mart store. People in
America have lamented for years that Wal-
Mart is scarring the face of hometown
America and turning one community into a
look-alike for every community.*[19]

According to the US pressure group Sprawl-Busters, Iowa
State University Professor Ken Stone examined the sales
changes in Iowa small towns from 1983 to 1993, a state
that in the ten years after Wal-Mart moved in lost:[20]

- 555 grocery stores

- 298 hardware stores

- 293 building supply stores

- 161 variety stores

- 158 women's clothes stores

- 153 shoe stores

- 116 drug stores

- 111 men and boys' clothes stores

Andy Rowel reports that for every $10 million in sales
in a typical Franklin County retail business, 106 people
are employed. For every $10 million sales at a Wal-
Mart, 70 people are employed. In other words, for every

job generated at Wal-Mart, one and a half jobs are lost elsewhere. In the town of Greenfield near Boston, despite Wal-Mart creating a promised 293 new jobs, the net impact of the store would be a gain of just 27 jobs, because of jobs lost from other businesses.[21]

Bob Ortega wrote in his book *In Sam We Trust: The Untold Story of Sam Walton and How Wal-Mart Is Devouring the World*:

> *Wal-Mart's executives have demonstrated an often-breathtaking contempt for laws and regulations. In the US, courts again and again have found the company to have lied, to have illegally falsified, destroyed and withheld documents, to have committed civil fraud, to have wilfully sold counterfeit goods, to have deliberately discriminated against disabled job applicants, to have illegally fired workers for interracial dating, to have discriminated against black and Mexican employees in other ways, to have allowed managers to sexually harass women workers - and to have fired women who had the temerity to complain.*[22]

The *Ecologist* magazine reported that factories producing clothes for Wal-Mart have consistently been found using forced or child labour. It reports that garments sewn by 12 year olds in Bangladesh for Wal-Mart stating 'Made in the USA'. The factory children were locked in at night until they had finished their production quotas.

Only a year before Wal-Mart had shifted production to the notorious Saraka factory in the country, 25 child workers had died in a fire at the facility, unable to escape. The *Ecologist* reported that in Honduras, the US based National Labour Committee (NLC) found that women as young as fourteen were employed in up to 14 hour daily shifts, with occasional mandatory 24-hour shifts. They had to work seven days a week, and if they could not, they would be fired. In 1999, the NLC released reports on the continuing use of sweatshop labour for clothes made for Wal-Mart in Honduras, Mexico, El Salvador, China, Bangladesh and Guatemala.[23]

The verdict

It is clear that the major supermarkets have pushed and bullied their way to enormous profit. As George Monbiot says in his book *Captive State*:

> *The key to much of their [supermarket] success lies not within the market but outside it. They enjoy more political influence than almost any other corporate sector in Britain. Their huge financial muscle helps them to bend both local and national government to their will. This political power appears to have enabled them to trade on terms that would surely not be tolerated in any other area of British commercial life. They offer convenience and choice in their stores only by destroying convenience and choice elsewhere.*[24]

The problem for society and the environment is that the most 'successful' model of a supermarket is Wal-Mart, but it is also accused of being the worst abuser of the environment, local communities, suppliers and its employees. There is something fundamentally wrong with the political and economic systems that allow this to happen. There is some hope; recently the European and UK parliaments have been trying to grapple this issue by drafting corporate responsibility legislation. Organisations such as the Corporate Responsibility Coalition (CORE) have been lobbying for this type of legislation for some time (see the table below). The proposed Corporate Responsibility Bill in the UK aims to:[25]

(a) Make companies report on any major impacts they have on the environment and on the communities in which they work, so that they measure and improve their impacts year on year.

(b) Give directors a 'duty of care' for their company's environmental and social impacts; not just a financial duty to provide profit for shareholders.

(c) Help ensure companies who damage the environment or communities abroad can be held liable in the UK.

The Corporate Responsibility Coalition (CORE)[26]

Basic human rights and the environment are being put at risk by the impacts of companies. The Corporate Responsibility Coalition (CORE) is pressing for binding rules in order to address this and protect the interests of vulnerable communities and the environment.

As part of an unprecedented movement to ensure companies meet their environmental and humanitarian responsibilities, Amnesty International, Christian Aid, Friends of the Earth, the New Economics Foundation, Traidcraft and the Unity Trust Bank have formed the CORE coalition to persuade the government to address the failures of the voluntary approach with binding rules for companies. Now supported by over 50 organisations, including non-governmental organisations, church groups and trade unions, CORE is demanding a common set of enforceable rules.

Website: www.foe.co.uk/campaigns/corporates/core

Chapter 8

Who Is to Blame?

Currently supermarkets control over two thirds of the grocery market. A handful of companies dominate where we buy our food and increasingly where we purchase other products such as electronics, books, clothes and pharmaceutical items. Is it their fault or ours? Are supermarkets simply the product of the society we live in, or have these enormous companies developed a life and momentum of their own, beyond our control?

The cost of supermarket shopping

One of the most common allegations against supermarkets is that they bully suppliers and farmers. With almost only the supermarkets to buy their products, suppliers and farmers have to deal with a relatively small numbers of buyers who have incredible influence over the market. The impact of this purchasing power has capped farm prices achieved through using direct contracting, rather than suppliers competing on price, and the use of (or threat to use) imports. Supermarkets switch their buyers around every six to twelve months to avoid relationships and loyalty to suppliers developing.[1]

Supermarkets have been accused of launching their own-label imitation of successful branded products, often using almost identical packaging and recipes and at lower prices. 'Category management' (where a leading supplier will control what goes on the supermarket shelf according to consumer demands) concerns some. These chosen suppliers have privileged access to the sales data of all suppliers of products in their category, and only the very largest suppliers have the resources to become category managers. Suppliers of fresh produce, meat products, dairy and bakery produce complained that supermarkets are selling their goods at a lower price, or even at a loss. Suppliers are concerned that below-cost selling could distort the price structure of whole product types (e.g. chocolate), and hence the mix of products bought. They are also worried that it puts enormous pressure on manufacturers to reduce prices to offset retailers' losses as consumers switch to products sold below cost. The supposed solution of a 'Code of Practice on Supermarkets' Dealings With Suppliers' has been widely seen as a failure.

With their large purchasing and marketing power, supermarkets have out-competed smaller independent stores. There has been a major decline in specialist, independent stores (butchers, bakers, greengrocers, etc); and a decline in the availability of local and regional produce. The loss of local facilities can lead to the creation of food and enterprise deserts, loss of employment, loss of outlets for local products and services, reduction of diversity of cultural and retail environments, and environmental impacts due to car-based shopping. The arrival of a supermarket has a huge impact on the viability of a rural community. It has been estimated that a supermarket opening will cause the closure of village shops within a seven-mile radius.[2] It is estimated that a community can expect to see a net loss of about 276 jobs once a supermarket moves into its area. Most of this will be from the small locally owned food shops.[3]

The supermarket system caters better for the time poor, cash rich than for the time poor, cash poor; for car owners than those dependent on buses. When food retailing left the high street, the poorest found themselves living in so-called 'food deserts' without adequate local food shops. Poor people tend to eat poor quality food (ie high in fat and sugar) because it is cheaper and is usually more filling. Poor families spend a higher proportion of their income on food – 27 per cent compared with 18 per cent – but this still amounts to less pounds per household in real terms. People in low-income households know which foods are healthy, but may be unable to buy them because they are unavailable, too expensive, or (in the case of perishable foods, such as fruit) they fear wastage. The cheapest calories come from the least nourishing foods (such as white bread and biscuits), and more nutritious foods have increased in price more steeply than less nutritious equivalents.[4]

Supermarkets alone generate 200,000 tonnes of compostable material every year, but encouraging the environ-mentally friendly disposal of such material has proved difficult.[5] 40 per cent or even as much as 50 per cent of raw vegetables or salad by weight may be rejected at various stages along a production line. Some hygienic and nourishing, substandard food products are available that may exhibit physical attributes considered 'flaws' by principal retailers.

Sustain report that the transport of food by air has

expanded significantly, and in the UK the distance that food was transported by road increased by 50 per cent between 1978 and 1999. The food system now accounts for between a third and 40 per cent of all UK road freight. A traditional meal, if bought at a supermarket, will have many ingredients imported and could have travelled, cumulatively, over 24,000 miles. However, choosing seasonal products and purchasing them locally at a farmers' market, for instance, could reduce the total distance to 376 miles.[6] The ideal supermarket, according to Sustain, would provide a window on local agriculture by achieving high levels of support for regional foods and local economies. To further the development of local sourcing, customers need to be presented with well-presented, accurate information and guidance.[7]

There is increasing evidence to suggest that the intensification of agriculture has damaged biodiversity, and there have been several instances of species becoming extinct. Agricultural landscapes with a low degree of variability have been developed, through specialisation and intensification. The use of artificial fertilisers and pesticides, combined with changes in groundwater tables, cropping patterns and stocking densities, have led to large scale losses or degradation of populations of domestic and wild species and agro-ecosystems.[8] Supermarkets can play a significant role in encouraging and supporting farmers who supply their produce to adopt more biodiversity and landscape-friendly practices, by integrating additional requirements into their existing farm assurance schemes.

Government tests for pesticide residues show that 46 per

cent of apples sold in supermarkets between 1998–2001 contained pesticide residues, and 18 per cent contained the residue of more than one pesticide.[9] The latest fashion in the supermarkets is organic food; although the stores have been criticised for overselling it for a large profit, using excess packaging and importing the majority, thus adding to food miles.[10] A seldom-mentioned impact of industrial agriculture is that it deprives consumers of real choice by favouring only a few varieties of crops that allow efficient harvesting, processing and packaging.[11]

Compassion in World Farming states that intensive agriculture in Europe and America has caused many problems: diseases, a diminished environment, poor welfare in farm animals and the decline of farming communities and rural livelihoods. The current crisis in European agriculture is largely borne out of the over-intensification of farm animals and crops. Supermarkets have enormous influence over animal-welfare standards. Supermarkets collectively represent the main conduit by which low-welfare animal products reach the general public.[12] Many of the world's (marine) fisheries are currently overexploited or have unacceptable impacts on the wider environment, according to the RSPB. Supermarkets currently source seafood products from all over the world, and it is a major challenge to establish whether the species they are sourcing and the fisheries, which supply these species, are sustainable and well managed.[13]

Hand in hand, the microwave and deep-freeze convenience foods, which gouge higher margins due to being 'value added' products, have all but eliminated the tradition of domestic cookery from British homes. Manufacturers and retailers have supported this process. The sales of convenience foods grew to £11bn in 2001, and have been projected to grow by 33 per cent in the next ten years.[14] Friends of the Earth, when looking at the special lines offered by supermarkets in a survey of Britain's leading supermarkets, found that the majority of items being promoted were fatty and sugary processed foods.[15] A Consumers' Association's survey of food labelling in 2003 revealed that children who eat a regular diet of foods specifically marketed with them in mind could face future health problems.[16] Almost all food advertisements aimed at children are for confectionery, sugary cereals, ready-prepared foods and fast-food outlets.[17] In an effort to put the consumer's mind at rest over the issue, Britain's major food companies, supermarkets and caterers launched a coalition in 2003 aimed at combating high rates of obesity in children. The move is being seen by campaigners as a belated attempt to fend off the imposition of much stricter regulations over food.[18]

Supermarket supply chains are like tentacles with a huge number of suppliers and sub-contractors extending in all directions and all over the world. According to Julie Smith in a report for the 'Race to the Top' super-market project, the supermarkets' drive to lower input costs and increase the amount and variety of food can, however, result in high social costs for the workers involved in the process.[19]

Corporate Watch points out that supermarkets employ large numbers of unskilled women, students, school children and disabled workers, often paying them on 'starter rates' so that, with the high staff turnover that is characteristic of some of these workers, labour costs are kept to a minimum. Furthermore, workers' rights, for example to decline to work on Sundays or vote on an annual pay rise, have been eroded in many cases.[20] Food is produced by workers from all over the world, many of who are working in poor conditions, for poor wages and with little or no protection from exploitation. Questions are increasingly being asked about the fairness of trade between consumers and the workers along the food chain. The rights of these workers, like the rights of workers in the UK, have become an issue that concern retailers, unions, consumers and shareholders of supermarket companies.[21]

Meanwhile, the selected few at the top of supermarkets stand accused of 'fat cat' salaries. Seven senior directors of Marks and Spencer shared more than £2.4m in bonuses last year, compared with the average annual bonus received by the 65,000 staff of a reported £624.[22] The executive directors at Tesco will receive a minimum of five years' salary under 'termination provisions' revealed for the first time this year as part of a complex 'executive incentive scheme'. This suggests that Sir Terry Leahy will receive five times his basic £916,000 salary – around £4.6m.[23]

The Competition Commission found that supermarkets were putting prices up in areas where there was no strong competition. Supermarkets have also been in trouble with the Advertising Standards Authority (ASA) on numerous occasions for misleading advertisements.[24] Government inquiries have only assessed whether supermarkets are monopolies or not on the basis of comparing places where people do their monthly or weekly shops, ie supermarkets. This only encourages a 'competitive' environment for the large supermarkets: there should be no less than five competing supermarkets in a local area according to the Safeway inquiry. This only saturates the market with national or international supermarket chains, providing no opportunity for local competition in the form of specialist shops, such as butchers, chemists or bakers, or local supermarkets.

Tesco is on a winning streak at the moment and Asda is doing very well – Sainsbury's and Safeway are struggling. Taking Safeway out of the equation by merging with Morrisons is not really going to make a radical difference to the market. But it is one fewer option facing the interesting but smallish food producer trying to get a product into national distribution. There is nothing we as individuals can do about the concentration of power in the supermarket, but we can keep the supermarkets on their toes by our daily shopping habits. We can use the corner stores. We can go to farmers' markets. We can buy our meat from real butchers who know about hanging meat in order to improve the taste. We can buy fair trade coffee. We can use the smaller chains that are doing something innovative or interesting rather than the giants. Consumers are the masters now, if we all but knew it.[25]

In 2003, the largest company in the world was a supermarket – Wal-Mart with $244 billion[26] worth of sales. It is seen as having the best and the worst of supermarket power:

> *For saving a few cents, we are supposed to sacrifice 20 to 30 acres of land, lose jobs in other stores, and support low-wage labour. It is a quality of life issue. You're surrounded by gridlock and the architectural graffiti of a windowless Wal-Mart store. People in America have lamented for years that Wal-Mart is scarring the face of hometown America and turning one community into a look-alike for every community.*
>
> Al Norman, *Slam-Dunking Wal-Mart – How You Can Stop Superstore Sprawl in Your Hometown.*[27]

Supermarket monopolies

The handful of major supermarkets that the majority of us shop at are very successful businesses. The consumer is delighted to be offered an incredible range of mostly cheap products; not just groceries but bank accounts, televisions, clothes, medicines, books, toys and so on. The list is endless. The supermarkets offer a lifestyle to suit every desire and consumers have rewarded the top supermarkets – some may say justly – with total domination of the market. So why attack supermarkets? In comparison with the tobacco, defence, biotechnology, nuclear, mining and petroleum industries, supermarkets have a clean, bright, friendly image.

The problem is that only four or five supermarkets control what we eat (and increasingly other aspects of our lives), and do it in such a ruthless manner that both society and the environment suffer. Food impacts on every aspect of our daily lives from health to socialising; it affects communities from jobs to regional identity; it affects the environment from shaping the landscape to waste; it affects workers from supermarket employees to farmers in developing countries; and, it affects other industries from biotechnology to farming. Just a handful of companies, essentially, pull all the strings. The supermarket format per se does not have to have such a negative influence. There are examples of positive actions by supermarkets such as Booths and the Co-operative Group, who have a philosophy of working with society not against it.

Essentially, supermarkets have an enormous responsibility as a result of the power they exercise over society. This responsibility is ignored as initiative after initiative fails to address the fundamental impacts of their operations. The government has reinforced the supermarkets' dominance, by either focusing on competition between the big supermarkets or treating supermarkets as shops and not as a hugely powerful industry. Inquiries have either addressed the wrong questions or just skated over the issues superficially. Pressure and consumer groups have fallen into the trap of dealing with specific impacts. Supermarkets affect society and the environment in numerous ways but, so far, no one has seriously addressed their fundamental stranglehold over society and the environment. Consumers do not see the connections between the death of local shops, congestion on the roads, packaging waste, food deserts and the farming crisis through their obsession with cheap, convenient shopping.

Supermarkets should recognise that their success has come at a terrible cost to society and the environment. The supermarket industry needs to radically change to untangle its web of actions. Supermarkets should address their impacts by changing from companies into organisations that care about their actions. But such management tools are only as good as the central goals, missions and philosophies of the supermarkets. Many supermarkets use management tools and initiatives such as environmental auditing, ethical trading, local sourcing and waste minimisation but only as marginal, bolt-on programmes. It is encouraging that these tolls and initiatives are being used, but it is not enough. Essentially, supermarkets need to bring society's values into the heart of their activities.

It is time that government, pressure groups and consumers also took responsibility for their actions and recognised that the supermarket industry should be held to account. These groups also need to accept some responsibility for the current situation. Government and civic society create the rules within which supermarkets operate. Consumers should realise that supermarkets are successful because they respond to consumer desires. Consumer desires could also create demands for a better society and environment; for example, with regards to the rejection of GM food, more regional produce and ethical trading.

An ethical supermarket?

A project between pressure groups and supermarkets called *Race to the Top* tried to rank all the major UK supermarkets' commitment to sustainable development, from energy usage and waste management, the treatment of their labour force, dealings with farmers, measures to protect the countryside and wildlife and promotion of animal welfare, to contributions to public health goals and support of local communities. The results showed that:

> *The Co-op emerged as the most ethical company leading UK supermarket in a wide-ranging study of supermarkets and sustainability. The Manchester-based Co-operative Group was best in class in six out of seven categories. Safeway showed leadership in the Environment category and performed well in other areas. Somerfield also demonstrated its commitment through an open willingness to be measured and monitored by its critics.* [28]

Unfortunately, only these three supermarkets (the Co-operative Group, Safeway and Somerfield) took part in the 2003 survey. Iceland, Marks and Spencer and Sainsbury's participated in the development of the indicators and a confidential pilot round of data collection in 2002, but declined to be ranked in 2003. Asda, Tesco, Waitrose and Morrisons chose not to participate. [29] When powerful companies do not want to disclose information this can only be interpreted as proving the case that the majority of the supermarket industry cannot be taking ethical issues seriously.

Consumer and government action

We all depend on supermarkets to provide most of our food and a range of other products under one roof because our busy lives dictate it. What can consumers do to stop the social and environmental destruction resulting from this shopping habit? Variety is the key. You do not have to completely kick the habit of super-market shopping, but instead focus on becoming more of a social shopper. Supermarkets depend on bread and milk to get customers through the doors on a regular basis. If you can get these products from other sources then suddenly you no longer automatically go to super-markets for your shopping. Buying your food from a variety of sources opens your shopping basket to real choice and makes food shopping a social event rather than a chore.

To lessen the impacts of supermarket shopping, follow these ten rules:

1. Be informed about the food you eat and the conditions under which they are produced by joining pressure groups such as Sustain or Friends of the Earth. Subscribe to maga-zines such as *Ethical Consumer,* the *Ecologist* or *New Internationalist.*

2. Know what is in the food you eat. Make more of your own meals from scratch rather than relying on ready meals.

3. Start buying food that has character and flavour without packaging or pesticides. Stop expecting fruit and vegetables to look 'supermarket' perfect.

4. Involve your children and family in food shopping and preparation as a social event rather than a duty.

5 Buy products labelled with the FAIRTRADE, Marine Stewardship Council or RSPCA logos.

6. Buy your fruit, vegetables, meat, dairy, bakery products and drinks locally and in season, or grow or make your own.

7. Try a local organic fruit and vegetable box scheme.

8. Ask your supermarket to stock local, regional and UK products, offer more variety, and more of the products with assured labels.

9. Demand clearer, more informative and honest labelling from your supermarket.

10. Ask your supermarket about its policies, targets and performance on the social and environmental issues you feel most strongly about.

The government also needs to take action to level the playing field for local shops:

1. The Department of Trade and Industry, the Office of Fair Trading and the Competition Commission should all include local retailers as competitors in their food-shopping surveys, which currently only see the large supermarkets as competitors.

2. Implement the Office of Fair Trading's Code of Practice on Supermarkets' Dealings with Suppliers into legislation.

3. Introduce grants and tax breaks to encourage local food markets such as farmers' markets and food produced under the label schemes such as the FAIRTRADE Mark.

4. Favour tax on aviation fuel, so that the environmental cost of flying food across the globe is included in the price.

5. Enforce the new phase (2004–2008) of the EC Directive on Packaging and Packaging

Waste, to achieve the targets set for businesses to recycle packaging.

6. Introduce a tax on plastic carrier bags.

7. Implement regulations for building or altering supermarket stores to include environmental features such as energy and water conservation as well as developments on previously used (brown field) sites or in existing buildings.

8. Force supermarkets to display their environmental and ethical-trading policies, and their procedures for dealing with suppliers in all stores, with annual performance against targets.

9. Implement the Corporate Responsibility Bill proposed by the Corporate Responsibility Coalition (CORE).

10. Start making realistic legislation that does not allow the exploitation of supermarket employees while the supermarket directors get 'fat cat' wages.

An alternative future?

A Europe-wide research project called SusHouse produced a theoretical scenario of an ideal food-shopping experience in 2050. Essentially, the vision is one where food is supplied from local, organic sources, eating habits are a mixture of conventional home cooking, visits to local eating-houses and other communal arrangements, and all food, whether domestic or retail, is purchased from corner shops or local farms. The story below illustrates how it would work. Happy shopping!

A story about the perfect shopping experience in 2050[30]

Jean had tried muesli before, but each time had quickly exchanged 'all that chewing' for her customary bacon and eggs. Peter and the kids were vegetarian, and though they still occasionally made a jibe at her for being a carnivore, they were generally more accepting of her choice now that the chickens and pigs were reared humanely just outside the city. The muesli was also produced locally, with the raisins and bananas swapped for plums and apples.

After breakfast, the kids did the dishes while Jean put on her police uniform and Peter made the children's packed lunch. The bread for the sandwiches was fresh from the bread-making machine and made with local organic flour. Peter slapped in some cheese that he'd picked up the day before from the small delicatessen adjacent to his work, adding a bag of red currants from their twice weekly delivery of organic fruit and vegetables and a piece of carrot cake from their local bakery. He couldn't resist nibbling a little bit of the cheese before putting it back in the cool room – it was so different to the bland, mass-produced cheese he'd been brought up with. This was real cheese, made from decent non-antibiotic milk in a local shop.

Previously, Peter had driven the kids to school, but since the onset of a 'local and green' policy, fewer large trucks used the road outside their house and so the kids were now able to walk. Shortly after the children left, Jean and Peter set off for work. While Peter walked, Jean caught a tram to the police station where she worked.

Who Is to Blame?

The kids were particularly enthusiastic about school today: in the afternoon they were going on a train out of the city, one for a biology class, and the other to go cross-country running. The school had begun such trips once they perceived the chemical risk from crop spraying had reduced. Previously, agriculture had lost much of its link with nature, becoming in many respects little more than an extension of the chemical industry. The shift to organic food had not only removed pesticide and other chemical residues from the food and the land, but had also re-established the links between farming and the public.

Though only a short, circular course, the cross-country run took the children past many different crops: vegetables grown under long rows of reusable plastic cloches, old-style orchards with a wide variety of apples, pears, plums and other traditional fruit, relatively small fields of different cereal crops separated by an intricate lattice of winding hedge rows, and several fields of high-tech greenhouses containing everything from tomatoes to apricots and kiwi fruit.

The biology lesson involved a walk around a farm showing the basics of an organic system: how physical barriers and natural systems ward off pests; the application of compost and manure rather than artificial fertilisers; the creation of smaller fields to mitigate soil erosion and encourage species diversity. They also discussed how the initially high production costs of regional organic foods had reduced as the scale of the system increased and a complementary transport and retail infrastructure developed, and

223

also how a closer relationship between agriculture and nature avoided such costly incidents as the BSE scare that had occurred at the end of the previous century.

Most evenings the children and the parents dined together; today, however, was Peter and Jean's wedding anniversary, so while they walked to their favourite restaurant, the kids ate at a friend's house. What had initially begun as a friendly arrangement between Peter, Jean and their immediate neighbours now included four families. Twice a week two sets of parents organised and cooked dinner for themselves and all the children. This system gave all the parents at least one evening to themselves each week, safe in the knowledge that their children were being well cared for. To the surprise of the families, two elderly couples had also joined the scheme, saying that they liked the feeling of community spirit. Certainly, in Jean's experience as a policewoman, she had noticed a significant reduction in crime since such communal schemes had become more widely adopted.

References

Preface

1   Policy Commission on the Future of Farming and Food (2002), 'Farming and food –
        a sustainable future', London: Cabinet Office [Source: www.cabinet-
        office.gov.uk/farming, Accessed 13/08/03], p.16.
2   Holden, J., Howland, L. & Stedman Jones, D. (2002), *Foodstuff – living in an age of
        feast and famine*, London: Demos, p.6.
3   McGavin, K. (2003), 'Checking out the supermarkets II – competition in retailing',
        London: Colin Breed, Liberal Democrats [Source:
        http://www.colinbreed.org.uk/downloads/CHECKINGOUTTHESUPERMARKET-
        SII.doc, Accessed: 05/08/03] p.4.
4   Riddell, M. (2003), 'We just can't keep out of supermarkets', the *Observer* (19 January
        2003), London, p.28.
5   *SN – Supermarket News* (2003), 'SN Global Top 25', New York: *Supermarket News*
        [Source: http://www.supermarketnews.com/sntop25.htm, Accessed: 03/10/03].
6   McGavin, K. (2003), p.4.

Chapter 1 - Who Are the Supermarkets?

1   *SN – Supermarket News* (2003), 'SN Global Top 25', New York: *Supermarket News*
        [Source: http://www.supermarketnews.com/sntop25.htm, Accessed: 03/10/03].
2   Seth, A. & Randall, G. (2001)(2nd Edition), *The Grocers – The Rise and Rise of
        Supermarket Chains*, London: Kogan Page, pp.6–7.
3   Seth, A. & Randall, G. (2001), p.7.
4   Seth, A. & Randall, G. (2001), pp.7–8
5   Seth, A. & Randall, G. (2001), pp.8–9.
6   Seth, A. & Randall, G. (2001), pp.16–18.
7   Seth, A. & Randall, G. (2001), p.19.
8   Seth, A. & Randall, G. (2001), p.20.
9   Adapted from Seth, A. & Randall, G. (2001), pp.19–20.
10   Guardian Unlimited (2003), 'Supermarkets – A chronology of key developments in
        the UK supermarket industry', London: Guardian Unlimited [Source:
        http://www.guardian.co.uk/supermarkets/story/0,12784,879400,00.html, Accessed
        22/10/03].
11   Adapted from Competition Commission (2003), 'Safeway plc and Asda Group
        Limited (owned by Wal-Mart Stores Inc); Wm Morrison Supermarkets PLC; J
        Sainsbury plc; and Tesco plc – A report on the mergers in contemplation', London:
        Department of Trade and Industry, pp.197–98.
12   Mintel (2002a), *Food Retailing in Europe 2002*, London: Mintel International Group Limited.

13   Figures from Mintel (2002b), *Food Retailing – UK – July 2002*, London: Mintel International Group Limited.

14   SN (2003).

15   Mintel (2002b).

16   Mintel (2002b).

17   Mintel (2002b).

18   Mintel (2002b).

19   Mintel (2002b).

20   Mintel (2002b).

21   Mintel (2002b).

22   Mintel (2002b).

23   Mintel (2002b).

24   Mintel (2002b).

25   Mintel (2002b).

26   Mintel (2002b).

27   Mintel (2002b).

28   Mintel (2002b).

29   Mintel (2002b).

30   Mintel (2002b).

31   Mintel (2002b).

32   Mintel (2003), *Clothing Retailing – UK – August 2003*, London: Mintel International Group Limited.

33   Mintel (2002b).

34   Mintel (2002b).

35   Mintel (2002b).

36   Mintel (2002b).

37   Mintel (2002b).

38   Mintel (2002b).

39   Mintel (2002b).

40   Mintel (2002b).

Chapter 2 - Suppliers and Farmers

1   McRae, H. (2003), 'Like them or not, supermarkets have improved our quality of life', the *Independent*, London [Source: http://argument.independent.co.uk/regular_columnists/hamish_mcrae/story.jsp?story=369238, Accessed: 06/02/03].

2   Vorley, B. (2002), 'Briefing Paper: Producers Module', *Race To The Top*, London: International Institute for Environment and Development [Source: www.racetothetop.org/indicators/mod ule2/page_7.htm#, Accessed: 03/08/03] pp.2–10.

3   Competition Commission (2000), 'Supermarkets – A report on the supply of groceries from multiple stores in the United Kingdom', London: Department of Trade and Industry, pp.65–66.

References

4   Figures from Competition Commission (2003), 'Safeway plc and Asda Group
        Limited (owned by Wal-Mart Stores Inc); Wm Morrison Supermarkets PLC; J
        Sainsbury plc; and Tesco plc – A report on the mergers in contemplation', London:
        Department of Trade and Industry, pp.172 & 242.
5   Competition Commission (2000), p.231.
6   Competition Commission (2000), pp.65–66.
7   Millstone, E. & Lang, T. (2003), *The Atlas of Food – Who Eats What, Where and Why*,
        London: Earthscan Publications Ltd, p.84.
8   Competition Commission (2000), pp.65–66.
9   Competition Commission (2000), p.231.
10   Competition Commission (2000), p.231.
11   Lang, T. (2003), 'The Saturday Essay', the *Grocer*, 14 June, p.34.
12   Competition Commission (2000), pp.65–66.
13   Competition Commission (2000), pp.234–38.
14   Competition Commission (2000), pp.234–38.
15   Competition Commission (2000), pp.234–38.
16   Vorley, B. (2002), pp.2–10.
17   Competition Commission (2000), pp.6–7.
18   Competition Commission (2000), p.98.
19   Competition Commission (2000), pp.6–7.
20   Competition Commission (2000), pp.140–43.
21   Competition Commission (2000), pp.234–38.
22   Competition Commission (2000), pp.234–38.
23   Competition Commission (2000), pp.234–38.
24   Competition Commission (2000), pp.240–41.
25   Competition Commission (2000), pp.240–41.
26   Competition Commission (2000), pp.242–44.
27   Competition Commission (2000), pp.242–44.
28   Competition Commission (2000), pp.242–44.
29   Competition Commission (2000), pp.242–44.
30   Competition Commission (2000), pp.242–44.
31   Competition Commission (2000), pp.242–44.
32   Competition Commission (2000), pp.242–44.
33   Friends of the Earth (2003), 'Briefing: Super markets or corporate bullies', London:
        Friends of the Earth [Source:
        http://www.foe.co.uk/resource/briefings/super_markets_corporate_bullies.pdf,
        Accessed: 12/05/03].
34   Friends of the Earth (2003).
35   Competition Commission (2000), pp.247–49.
36   Competition Commission (2000), pp.247–49.
37   Competition Commission (2000), pp.247–49.
38   Competition Commission (2000), pp.247–49.
39   Competition Commission (2000), pp.247–49.
40   Competition Commission (2000), pp.258–59.

41   Vorley, B. (2002), pp.2–10.

42   Vorley, B. (2002), pp.2–10.

43   Vorley, B. (2002), pp.2–10.

44   Vorley, B. (2002), pp.2–10.

45   Vorley, B. (2002), pp.2–10.

46   Vorley, B. (2002), pp.2–10.

47   Vorley, B. (2002), pp.2–10.

48   Vorley, B. (2002), pp.2–10.

49   Vorley, B. (2002), pp.2–10.

50   National Farmers' Union (2002), 'Counting the Ways that Farming Counts', London: National Farmers' Union [Source: www.nfu.org.uk/info/fcmarket.asp accessed 14 February 2003].

51   Vorley, B. (2002), pp.2–10.

52   Vorley, B. (2002), pp.2–10.

53   Adapted from DEFRA (2002), p.61.

54   DEFRA (2002), 'Farming and Food's Contribution to Sustainable Development – Economic and Statistical Analysis', London: Department for Environment, Food and Rural Affairs, p.14.

55   DEFRA (2002), p.54.

56   Vorley, B. (2002), pp.2–10.

57   Vorley, B. (2002), pp.2–10.

58   Adapted from Vorley, B. (2002), pp.2–10.

59   Vorley, B. (2002), pp.2–10.

60   Vorley, B. (2002), pp.2–10.

61   Vorley, B. (2002), pp.2–10.

62   Friends of the Earth (2003).

63   Vorley, B. (2002), pp.2–10.

64   Office of Fair Trading (2001), 'Code of Practice on Supermarkets' Dealings with Suppliers', London: Department of Trade and Industry [Source: www.dti.gov.uk/ccp/topics2/pdf2/codeofpractice.pdf accessed 3 March 2003].

65   Vorley, B. (2002), pp.2–10.

66   Bell, S. (2003), 'Farmers and the Supermarket Code of Practice', London: Friends of the Earth [Source: www.foe.co.uk, Accessed: 20 March 2003].

67   Bell, S. (2003).

68   Friends of the Earth (2003).

69   Friends of the Earth (2003).

70   Friends of the Earth (2003).

71   Fletcher, R. (2003), 'Safeway staff cash in shares ahead of OFT ruling on bids', the *Sunday Telegraph* – Business Section, London, 9 February 2003, p.2.

72   Friends of the Earth (2003).

73   Competition Commission (2000), pp.234–38.

74   Competition Commission (2003), p.239.

75   Competition Commission (2003), pp.239–41.

76   Vorley, B. (2002), pp.2–10.

Chapter 3 - Communities

1   McGavin, K. (2003), 'Checking out the supermarkets II – competition in retailing',
     London: Colin Breed, Liberal Democrats [Source:
     http://www.colinbreed.org.uk/downloads/CHECKINGOUTTHE SUPERMAR
     KETSII.doc, Accessed: 05/08/03] p.11.

2   Simms, A., Oram, J., MacGillivray A. & Drury, J. (2002), *Ghost Town Britain –
     The Threat from Economic Globalisation to Livelihoods, Liberty and Local
     Economic Freedom*, London: New Economics Foundation [Source:
     http://www.neweconomics.org/gen/uploads/ghost_town.pdf, Accessed 08/08/03]
     pp.2–3.

3   Simms, A., Oram, J., MacGillivray A. & Drury, J. (2002), pp.2–3.

4   Hird, V. & Shub, M. (2002), 'Briefing Paper: Communities Module', *Race To The
     Top*, London: International Institute for Environment and Development [Source:
     www.racetothetop.org/indicators/module4/page_7.htm#, Accessed: 03/08/03]
     pp.2–6

5   Friends of the Earth (2003), 'Briefing: Super markets or corporate bullies',
     London: Friends of the Earth [Source:
     http://www.foe.co.uk/resource/briefings/super_markets_corporate_bullies.pdf,
     Accessed: 12/05/03].

6   McGavin, K. (2003), p.11–12.

7   Hird, V. & Shub, M. (2002), pp.2–6.

8   Kirby, T. (2002), 'Tesco eats up corner shops in threat to local traders', the
     Independent, London: Independent.co.uk [Source:
     http://news.independent.co.uk/business/news/story.jsp?story=347447, accessed:
     04/11/02].

9   Simms, A., Oram, J., MacGillivray A. & Drury, J. (2002), pp.2–3.

10   Simms, A., Oram, J., MacGillivray A. & Drury, J. (2002), pp.2–3.

11   Simms, A., Oram, J., MacGillivray A. & Drury, J. (2002), pp.2–3.

12   Simms, A., Oram, J., MacGillivray A. & Drury, J. (2002), pp.2–3.

13   Hird, V. & Shub, M. (2002), pp.2–6.

14   Hird, V. & Shub, M. (2002), pp.2–6.

15   Simms, A., Oram, J., MacGillivray A. & Drury, J. (2002), pp.14–15.

16   Simms, A., Oram, J., MacGillivray A. & Drury, J. (2002), pp.14–15.

17   Rowell, A. (2000), 'SUCKERS – Why Britain Can't Afford Wal-Mart', the *Ecologist*,
     22/09/2000 [Source:
     http://www.andyrowell.com/articles/suckers_walmart.html,
     Accessed: 11/09/03].

18   Hird, V. & Shub, M. (2002), pp.2–6.

19   Simms, A., Oram, J., MacGillivray A. & Drury, J. (2002), pp.14–15.

20   Rowell, A. (2000), pp.14–15.

21   Hird, V. & Shub, M. (2002), pp.2–6.

22   Rowell, A (2000), pp.14–15.

23   Hird, V. & Shub, M. (2002), pp.2–6.

24 Sharpe, R. (2002), 'Briefing Paper: Health Module', *Race To The Top*, London: International Institute for Environment and Development [Source: www.racetothetop.org/indicators/module7/page_7.htm#, Accessed: 03/08/03], pp.2–8.

25 Hitchman, C., Christie, I., Harrison, M. & Lang, T. (2002), *Inconvenience food – the struggle to eat well on a low income*, London: Demos, pp.14–15.

26 Sharpe, R. (2002), pp.2–8.

27 Sharpe, R. (2002), pp.2–8.

28 Sharpe, R. (2002), pp.2–8.

29 Sharpe, R. (2002), pp.5–6.

30 Sharpe, R. (2002), pp.2–8.

31 Sharpe, R. (2002), pp.2–8.

32 Sharpe, R. (2002), pp.2–8.

33 Sharpe, R. (2002), pp.2–8.

34 Tesco (2003), 'Every little helps. Corporate Social Responsibility. Communities. Regeneration'. London: Tesco.com [Source: http://www.tesco.com/everylittlehelps/, Accessed 10/11/03].

Chapter 4 - The Environment

1 Howes, R. (2002), 'Briefing Paper: Environment Module', *Race To The Top*, London: International Institute for Environment and Development [Source: www.racetothetop.org/indicators/module1/page_7.htm#, Accessed: 03/08/03] pp.9–10.

2 Bruce, A. (2003), 'The waste time bomb', the *Grocer*, Vol 226, No. 7631, November 22, p.33.

3 McGavin, K. (2003), 'Checking Out the Supermarkets II – Competition in Retailing', London: Colin Breed, Liberal Democrats, [Source: http://www.colinbreed.org.uk/downloads/CHECKINGOUTTHESUPERMARKETSII.doc, Accessed: 05/08/03].

4 McGavin, K. (2003), pp.15–16.

5 Jones, A. (2001), *Eating Oil – Food Supply in a Changing Climate*, London: Sustain and Elm Farm Research Centre, p.1.

6 Bruce, A. (2003), p.33.

7 Hyde, K., Smith, A., Smith, M. & Henningsson, S. (2001), 'The challenge of waste minimisation in the foods and drink industry: a demonstration project in East Anglia, UK', *Journal of Cleaner Production*, No. 9, pp.57–58.

8 Bruce, A. (2003), p.33.

9 Howes, R. (2002), pp.9–10.

10 McGavin, K. (2003), pp.15–16.

11 McGavin, K. (2003), pp.15–16.

12 Bartram, H. (2002), 'Briefing Paper: Nature Module', *Race To The Top*, London: International Institute for Environment and Development [Source: www.racetothetop.org/indicators/module5/page_7.htm#, Accessed: 03/08/03] pp.2–3.

13 Bartram, H. (2002), p.4.

References

14   Bartram, H. (2002), p.4.

15   Vorley, B. (2002), 'Briefing Paper: Producers Module', *Race To The Top*, London: International Institute for Environment and Development [Source: www.racetothetop.org/indicators/module2/page_7.htm#, Accessed: 03/08/03] pp.2–10.

16   Bartram, H. (2002), p.6.

17   Bartram, H. (2002), p.6.

18   Bartram, H. (2002), pp.2–3.

19   Friends of the Earth (2003), 'Briefing: Super markets or corporate bullies', London: Friends of the Earth [Source: http://www.foe.co.uk/resource/brief-ings/super_markets_corporate_bullies.pdf, Accessed: 12/05/03].

20   Friends of the Earth (2003).

21   Howes, R. (2002), pp.7–8.

22   Howes, R. (2002), pp.7–8.

23   Jones, A. (2001), p.1.

24   Friends of the Earth (2003).

25   Friends of the Earth (2003).

26   Friends of the Earth (2003).

27   Jones, A. (2001), p.1.

28   Jones, A. (2001), p.1.

29   Jones, A. (2001), p.1.

30   Jones, A. (2001), p.1.

31   Jones, A. (2001), p.1.

32   Policy Commission on the Future of Farming and Food (2002), *Farming and food – a sustainable future*, Cabinet Office, London [Source: www.cabinet-office.gov.uk/farming, Accessed 13/08/03] p.92.

33   Friends of the Earth (2003).

34   Simms, A., Oram, J., MacGillivray A. & Drury, J. (2002), *Ghost Town Britain – The Threat from Economic Globalisation to Livelihoods, Liberty and Local Economic Freedom*, London: New Economics Foundation [Source: http://www.neweconomics.org/gen/uploads/ghost_town.pdf, Accessed 08/08/03] pp.14–15.

35   Friends of the Earth (2003).

36   Sustain (2001), *Sign Up for Your Climate Change Loyalty Card!* London: Sustain, [Source: http://www.sustainweb.org/pdf/eatoil_pr.PDF, Accessed 05/08/03] pp.1–2.

37   Jones, A. (2001) p.65.

38   Hird, V. & Shub, M. (2002), 'Briefing Paper: Communities Module', *Race To The Top*, London: International Institute for Environment and Development [Source: www.racetothetop.org/indicators/module4/page_7.htm#, Accessed: 03/08/03] pp.2–6.

39   Hird, V. & Shub, M. (2002), pp.2–6.

40   Hird, V. & Shub, M. (2002), pp.2–6.

41   Hird, V. & Shub, M. (2002), pp.2–6.

42   Hird, V. & Shub, M. (2002), pp.7–8.

43   Hird, V. & Shub, M. (2002), pp.7–8.

44   Hird, V. & Shub, M. (2002), pp.7–8.

45   Simms, A., Oram, J., MacGillivray A. & Drury, J. (2002), pp.14–15.

46   Hird, V. & Shub, M. (2002), pp.7–8.

47   Hird, V. & Shub, M. (2002), pp.7–8.

48   Lymbery, P. (2002), 'Briefing Paper: Animals Module', *Race To The Top*, London: International Institute for Environment and Development [Source: www.racetothetop.org/indicators/module6/page_7.htm#, Accessed: 03/08/03] pp.2–6.

49   Lymbery, P. (2002), pp.2–6.

50   Lymbery, P. (2002), pp.2–6.

51   Lymbery, P. (2002), pp.2–6.

52   Lymbery, P. (2002), pp.2–6.

53   Lymbery, P. (2002), pp.2–6.

54   Lymbery, P. (2002), pp.2–6.

55   Lymbery, P. (2002), pp.2–6.

56   Lymbery, P. (2002), pp.2–6.

57   DEFRA (2002), *Farming and Food's Contribution to Sustainable Development – Economic and Statistical Analysi*s, London: Department for Environment, Food and Rural Affairs, pp.39–40.

58   DEFRA (2002), pp.39–40.

59   DEFRA (2002), pp.39–40.

60   Bartram, H. (2002), pp.10–13.

61   Bartram, H. (2002), pp.10–13.

62   Bartram, H. (2002), pp.10–13.

63   Bartram, H. (2002), pp.10–13.

64   Bartram, H. (2002),) pp.10–13.

65   Bartram, H. (2002),) pp.10–13.

66   Bartram, H. (2002),) pp.2–3.

67   Carrell, S. (2003), 'Green group ejects Tesco over illegal wood', the *Independent on Sunday*, London, 3 August, p.15.

68   Grocer (2003), 'Agency's rebuke unfair says Tesco', the *Grocer*, Vol: 226, No 7615, August 2, p.10.

69   J Sainsbury plc (2002), *J. Sainsbury plc – Environmental Report 2002*, London: J Sainsbury plc [Source: http://www.j-sainsbury.co.uk/csr/envrep2002/frameset.cfm?page=performance_products, Accessed: 21/11/03].

70   Co-op (2002), *Consumer issues – Co-op Brand Packaging – Degradable and Biodegradable Technologies*, Manchester: The Co-operative Group [Source: http://www.co-op.co.uk/, Accessed: 21/11/03].

References

Chapter 5 - Supermarket Food

1   Millstone, E. & Lang, T. (2003), *The Atlas of Food – Who Eats What, Where and Why*, London: Earthscan Publications Ltd, p.84.

2   Bunyard, P. (2002), 'The agricultural cost of cheap supermarket food', the *Ecologist*, 22 March [Source: http://www.theecologist.org/archive_articles.html?category=52, Accessed 14/4/03].

3   DEFRA (2002), *Farming and Food's Contribution to Sustainable Development – Economic and Statistical Analysis*, London: Department for Environment, Food and Rural Affairs, p.9.

4   Bunyard, P. (2002).

5   Kimbrell, A. (2002) (Ed.), *The Fatal Harvest Reader – The Tragedy of Industrial Agriculture*, Washington: Island Press.

6   Kimbrell, A. (2002), p.6.

7   Kimbrell, A. (2002), p.10.

8   Kimbrell, A. (2002), p.15.

9   Kimbrell, A. (2002), p.19.

10   Kimbrell, A. (2002), p.23.

11   Kimbrell, A. (2002), p.28.

12   Kimbrell, A. (2002), p.32.

13   Blythman, J. (2003), 'Bite the dust', the *Guardian: Food – The way we eat now*, Issue 1, May 10, London, p.25.

14   Blythman, J. (2003).

15   Friends of the Earth (2002b). 'Briefing: Pesticides in supermarket food', London: Friends of the Earth [Source: http://www.foe.co.uk/resource/briefings/pesticides_supermkt_food.pdf, Accessed: 17/07/03].

16   Friends of the Earth (2002b).

17   Friends of the Earth (2002b).

18   Soil Association (2003a), 'Key Elements of Organic Farming', Bristol: Soil Association [Source: http://www.soilassociation.org/web/sa/saweb.nsf/Library?OpenForm&Cat=_Briefing_Sheets, Accessed: 29/07/03].

19   Soil Association (2003b), 'Organic food: facts and figures 2003', Bristol: Soil Association [Source: http://www.soilassociation.org/web/sa/saweb.nsf/Library?OpenForm&Cat=_Briefing_Sheets, Accessed: 13/11/03].

20   Friends of the Earth (2002c), 'Supermarkets Failing to Buy UK Organic Produce', London: Friends of the Earth [Source: http://www.foe.co.uk/resource/press_releases/20020725000130.html, Accessed: 13/11/03].

21   Adapted from GM Public Debate Steering Board (2003a), *GM Nation? The Public Debate – Section 1: Where do I start?* London: Department of Trade and Industry, [Source: http://www.gmpublicdebate.org/docs/gm_01.pdf, Accessed: 29/07/03], pp.1–3 & 7–9.

22   GM Public Debate Steering Board (2003b), *The findings of the public debate*, London: Department of Trade and Industry [Source: http://www.gmpublicdebate.org/ut_09/ut_9_6.htm, Accessed: 13/11/03].

23   Kimbrell, A. (2002), pp.23–27.

24   Mathiason, N. (2003), 'EU to end five-year ban on new GM products', the *Observer* – business, London, 16 November 2003, p.2.

25   Kimbrell, A. (2002), pp.23–27.

26   Kimbrell, A. (2002), pp.23–27.

27   Kimbrell, A. (2002), pp.23–27.

28   Kimbrell, A. (2002), pp.23–27.

29   Friends of the Earth (2003), 'Briefing: Super markets or corporate bullies', London: Friends of the Earth [Source: http://www.foe.co.uk/resource/briefings/super_markets_corporate_bullies.pdf, Accessed: 12/05/03].

30   Bartram, H. (2002), 'Briefing Paper: Nature Module', *Race To The Top*, London: International Institute for Environment and Development [Source: www.racetothetop.org/indicators/module5/page_7.htm#, Accessed: 03/08/03] pp.8–9.

31   Bartram, H. (2002), pp.8–9.

32   Kimbrell, A. (2002), pp.23–27.

33   Kimbrell, A. (2002), pp.23–27.

34   Kimbrell, A. (2002), pp.23–27.

35   Friends of the Earth (2003).

36   Dalmeny, K. (2003), 'Food marketing: the role of advertising in child health', *Consumer Policy Review*, Vol 13, Number 1, p.2.

37   Friends of the Earth (2003).

38   DEFRA (2002), pp.36–37.

39   DEFRA (2002), pp.36–37.

40   Sharpe, R. (2002), 'Briefing Paper: Health Module,' *Race To The Top*. London: International Imstitute for Environment and Development [Source: www.racetothetop.org/indicators/module7/page_7.htm#, Accessed: 03/08/03] pp.2–8.

41   DEFRA (2002), pp.36–37.

42   Policy Commission on the Future of Farming and Food (2002), p.102.

43   Meikle, J. (2003), 'Healthy food scheme spurned by major chains', the *Guardian*, London, 24 March.

44   Meikle, J. (2003).

45   Vorley, B. (2002), 'Briefing Paper: Producers Module', *Race To The Top*, London: International Institute for Environment and Development [Source: www.racetothetop.org/indicators/module2/page_7.htm#, Accessed: 03/08/03] pp.2–10.

46   Vorley, B. (2002), pp.2–10.

47   Vorley, B. (2002), pp.2–10.

48   Vorley, B. (2002), pp.2–10.

49   Vorley, B. (2002), pp.2–10.

50   Vorley, B. (2002), pp.2–10.

51   Dalmeny, K. (2003), 'Food marketing: the role of advertising in child health', *Consumer Policy Review*, Vol 13, Number 1, p.2.

52   Dalmeny, K. (2003), p.2

53   Friends of the Earth (2003).

54   Dalmeny, K. (2003), p.3

55   Consumers' Association (2003), 'Children who regularly eat 'kids' foods' could seriously damage their health', London: Consumers' Association [Source: http://www.which.net/media/pr/nov03/general/kidsfood.html, Accessed: 05/11/03].

56   *Grocer* (2003), 'Parents resilient to ad pressures', the *Grocer*, Crawley: William Reed Publishing, 30 August, p.10.

57   Smithers, R. (2003), 'Parents target sweets at tills', the *Guardian*, London, 20 October, p.5.

58   Revill, J. (2003), 'Food giants join Britain's war on flab', the *Observer*, London: the *Observer*, 16 November, p.5.

59   Revill, J. (2003). p.5.

60   *Guardian* (2003), '20 Ways to Change the Food System', the *Guardian: Food – The way we eat now*, Issue 1, May 10, London, p.32.

Chapter 6 – Employees and Workers

1   Smith, J. (2002), 'Briefing Paper: Workers Module', *Race To The Top*, London: International Institute for Environment and Development [Source: www.racetothetop.org/indicators/module3/page_7.htm#, Accessed: 03/08/03] pp.10–13.

2   Smith, J. (2002), pp.3–4.

3   McGavin, K. (2003), 'Checking out the supermarkets II – competition in retailing', London: Colin Breed, Liberal Democrats, [Source: http://www.colinbreed.org.uk/downloads/CHECKINGOUTTHESUPERMARKETSII.doc,], pp.12–13.

4   Gumbel, A. (2003), 'Wal-Mart faces prosecution over use of illegal workers', the *Independent*, London, 6 November 2003, p.18.

5   McGavin, K. (2003), pp.12–13.

6   McGavin, K. (2003), pp.12–13.

7   BBC News (2002), 'Union declares war on Wal-Mart', BBC News, London, 20 November, [Source: http://news.bbc.co.uk/1/hi/world/americas/2496357.stm, Accessed: 21/02/03].

8   BBC News (2002).

9   Smith, J. (2002), pp.5–7.

11   Smith, J. (2002), pp.5–7.

12   Smith, J. (2002), pp.5–7.

13   Smith, J. (2002), pp.5–7.

14   Smith, J. (2002), pp.5–7.

15   Smith, J. (2002), pp.5–7.

16   Smith, J. (2002), pp.5–7.

17   Smith, J. (2002), pp.5–7.

18   TUC (2003), 'Closing the Gender Poverty Gap', London: Trade Union Congress (TUC) [Source: http://www.tuc.org.uk/equality/tuc-6377-f0.cfm, Accessed: 26/01/03].

19   Smith, J. (2002), pp.10–13.

20   Environment, Food and Rural Affairs Select Committee (2003), 'Report Published on Gangmasters', London: The United Kingdom Parliament [Source: http://www.parliament.uk/parliamentary_committees/environment__food_and_rural_affairs/efra_pn80_030918.cfm, Accessed: 10/09/03].

21   Environment, Food and Rural Affairs Select Committee (2003).

22   Environment, Food and Rural Affairs Select Committee (2003).

23   Barrett, H.R., Ilbery, B.W., Browne, A.W & Binns, T. (1999), 'Globlization and the changing networks of food supply: the importation of fresh horticultural produce from Kenya into the UK', *Transactions: Institute of British Geographers*, 24, p.167.

24   Smith, J. (2002), pp.10–13

25   Young, W. & Welford, R. (2002), *Ethical Shopping: Where to Shop, What to Buy and What to do to Make a Difference*, London: Fusion Press, pp.18–22.

26   Young, W. & Welford, R. (2002), pp.18–22.

27   Young, W. & Welford, R. (2002), pp.18–22.

28   Young, W. & Welford, R. (2002), pp.18–22.

29   Smith, J. (2002), pp.3–4.

30   Smith, J. (2002), pp.10–13.

31   Smith, J. (2002), pp.10–13.

32   Smith, J. (2002), pp.10–13.

33   Vorley, B. (2002), 'Briefing Paper: Producers Module', *Race To The Top*, London: International Institute for Environment and Development [Source: www.racetothetop.org/indicators/module2/page_7.htm#, Accessed: 03/08/03] pp.2–10.

34   Young, W. & Welford, R. (2002), pp.24–26.

35   Young, W. & Welford, R. (2002), pp.24–26.

36   Young, W. & Welford, R. (2002), pp.24–26.

37   Young, W. & Welford, R. (2002), pp.24–26.

38   Young, W. & Welford, R. (2002), pp.24–26.

39   Clark, A. (2003), 'It's a flat-out life of luxury for M&S chair', the *Guardian*, London, 10 February, p.21.

40   *Guardian*, (2003), 'M&S largesse', the *Guardian*, London, 14 June.

41   Treanor, J. (2003), 'Tesco: next target in payoffs campaign', the *Guardian*, London, 3 June, p.14.

42   Finch, J. (2003), 'The great supermarket takeaway', the *Guardian*, London, 14 June, p.26.

Chapter 7 - Supermarkets' Abuse of Power

1   Friends of the Earth (2003a), 'Briefing: Super markets or corporate bullies', London: Friends of the Earth [Source: http://www.foe.co.uk/resource/briefings/super_markets_corporate_bullies.pdf, Accessed: 12/05/03].

References

2   Friends of the Earth (2003a).

3   Friends of the Earth (2003a).

4   Adapted from Friends of the Earth (2002), 'Press Briefing: British Apples For Sale –
        Markets and Greengrocers Have More for Less', London: Friends of the Earth
        [Source: http://www.foe.co.uk/resource/briefings/british_apples_for_sale.pdf, Accessed
        17/07/03].

5   *Grocer* (2003), 'Warning over Pharmacies', the *Grocer*, Crawley: William Reed
        Publishing, 21 June, p.11.

6   Competition Commission (2000), *Supermarkets – A report on the supply of groceries
        from multiple stores in the United Kingdom*, London: Department of Trade and
        Industry, pp.242–44.

7   Dolan, C. & Humphrey, J. (2000), 'Governance and Trade in Fresh Vegetables: The
        Impact of UK Supermarkets on the African Horticulture Industry', *Journal of
        Development Studies*, 37, (2), p.155.

8   Dolan, C. & Humphrey, J. (2000), p.155.

9   Simms, A., Oram, J., MacGillivray A. & Drury, J. (2002), *Ghost Town Britain – The
        Threat from Economic Globalisation to Livelihoods, Liberty and Local Economic Freedom*,
        London: New Economics Foundation [Source:
        http://www.neweconomics.org/gen/uploads/ghost_town.pdf, Accessed 08/08/03], p.35.

10   BBC News (2003), 'Your Politics: Supermarkets', London: BBC [Source:
        http://news.bbc.co.uk/1/hi/talking_point/forum/your_politics/2806011.stm,
        Accessed: 25/11/03].

11   Monbiot, G. (2000), *Captive State – The Corporate Takeover of Britain*, London:
        Macmillan, pp.195–196.

12   *Grocer Today* (2003), Press round-up....Safeway: 10/02/03, London: *Grocer Today*
        [Source: www.grocertoday.co.uk accessed 10 February 2003].

13   Friends of the Earth (2003b), 'Press Release: Safeway stitch up must be stopped,
        alliance demands', London: Friends of the Earth [Source:
        www.foe.co.uk/resource/press_releases/SAFEWAY_STITCH_UP_MUST_BE.html,
        Accessed: 10/02/03].

14   *NCC (2003)*, 'NCC News – 2/2/03 – Real choice for shoppers must determine super-
        market bids – National Consumer Council urges Competition inquiry', London:
        National Consumer Council [Source:
        http://ncc.keymedia.info/cgi-bin/kmdb10.cgi/-load103673_viewcurrent.htm,
        Accessed: 10/02/03].

15   Treanor, J. (2003), 'Sainsbury's drops shopping list', the *Guardian*, London: Guardian
        Unlimited [Source: http://www.guardian.co.uk/business/story/0,3604,1028095,00.html,
        Accessed: 02/09/03].

16   Treanor, J. (2003).

17   Michaels, L. (2002), *Whats wrong with supermarkets*, Oxford: Corporate Watch,
        pp.5–6.

18   Friends of the Earth (2003c), 'Ten Reasons Supermarket Mergers are Bad for
        Consumers', London: Friends of the Earth [Source:
        http://www.foe.co.uk/resource/press_releases/20030113134910.html, Accessed: 10/02/03].

19   Rowell, A. (2000).

20   Rowell, A. (2000).

21   Rowell, A. (2000).

22   Rowell, A. (2000).

23   Rowell, A. (2000).

24   Monbiot, G. (2000), *Captive State – The Corporate Takeover of Britain*, London: Macmillan, pp.195–96.

25   Friends of the Earth (2003c).

26   Friends of the Earth (2003c).

Chapter 8 - Who is to Blame?

1   Competition Commission (2000), *Safeway plc and Asda Group Limited (owned by Wal-Mart Stores Inc); Wm Morrison Supermarkets PLC; J Sainsbury plc; and Tesco plc – A report on the mergers in contemplation*, London: Department of Trade and Industry, p.98.

2   Friends of the Earth (2003), 'Briefing: Super markets or corporate bullies', London: Friends of the Earth [Source: http://www.foe.co.uk/resource/briefings/super_markets_corporate_bullies.pdf, Accessed: 12/05/03].

3   Simms, A., Oram, J., MacGillivray A. & Drury, J. (2002), *Ghost Town Britain – The Threat from Economic Globalisation to Livelihoods, Liberty and Local Economic Freedom*, London: New Economics Foundation [Source: http://www.neweconomics.org/gen/uploads/ghost_town.pdf, Accessed 08/08/03], pp.14–15.

4   Sharpe, R. (2002), 'Briefing Paper: Health Module', *Race To The Top*, London: International Institute for Environment and Development [Source: www.racetothetop.org/indicators/module7/page_7.htm#, Accessed: 03/08/03], pp.2–8.

5   McGavin, K. (2003), 'Checking out the supermarkets II – competition in retailing', London: Colin Breed, Liberal Democrats [Source: http://www.colinbreed.org.uk/downloads/CHECKINGOUTTHESUPERMAR-KETSII.doc, Accessed: 05/08/03], pp.15–16.

6   Sustain (2001), *Sign Up for Your Climate Change Loyalty Card!* London: Sustain [Source: http://www.sustainweb.org/pdf/eatoil_pr.PDF, Accessed 05/08/03], pp.1–2.

7   Hird, V. & Shub, M. (2002), 'Briefing Paper: Communities Module', *Race To The Top*, London: International Institute for Environment and Development [Source: www.racetothetop.org/indicators/module4/page_7.htm#, Accessed: 03/08/03], pp.7–8.

8   Bartram, H. (2002), 'Briefing Paper: Nature Module', *Race To The Top*, London: International Institute for Environment and Development [Source: www.racetothetop.org/indicators/module5/page_7.htm#, Accessed: 03/08/03] p.4.

9   Friends of the Earth (2003).

10   Friends of the Earth (2002a), 'Supermarkets Failing to Buy UK Organic Produce', London: Friends of the Earth [Source: http://www.foe.co.uk/resource/press_releases/20020725000130.html, Accessed: 13/11/03].

References

11   Kimbrell, A. (2002) (Ed.), *The Fatal Harvest Reader – The Tragedy of Industrial Agriculture*, Washington: Island Press, pp.23–27.

12   Lymbery, P. (2002), 'Briefing Paper: Animals Module', *Race To The Top*, London: International Institute for Environment and Development [Source: www.racetothetop.org/indicators/module6/page_7.htm#, Accessed: 03/08/03] pp.2–6.

13   Bartram, H. (2002), pp.10–13.

14   Fort, M. (2003), 'The Death of Cooking', the *Guardian: Food – The way we eat now*, Issue 1, May 10, London, p.11.

15   Friends of the Earth (2003).

16   Consumers' Association (2003), 'Children who regularly eat 'kids' foods' could seriously damage their health', London: Consumers' Association [Source: http://www.which.net/media/pr/nov03/general/kidsfood.html, Accessed: 05/11/03].

17   Dalmeny, K. (2003), 'Food marketing: the role of advertising in child health', *Consumer Policy Review*, Vol 13, Number 1, p.3.

18   Revill, J. (2003), 'Food giants join Britain's war on flab', the *Observer*, London, 16 November, p.5.

19   Smith, J. (2002), 'Briefing Paper: Workers Module', *Race To The Top*, London: International Institute for Environment and Development [Source: www.racetothetop.org/indicators/module3/page_7.htm#, Accessed: 03/08/03] pp.10–13

20   McGavin, K. (2003), *Checking out the supermarkets II – competition in retailing*, London: Colin Breed, Liberal Democrats [Source: http://www.colinbreed.org.uk/downloads/CHECKINGOUTTHESUPERMARKETSII.doc, Accessed: 05/08/03] pp.12–13.

21   Smith, J. (2002), pp.2–3.

22   *Guardian*, (2003), 'M&S largesse', the *Guardian*, London,14 June, p.26.

23   Treanor, J. (2003), 'Tesco: next target in payoffs campaign', the *Guardian*, London, 3 June, p.14.

24   Friends of the Earth, (2003).

25   McRae, H. (2003), 'Like them or not, supermarkets have improved our quality of life', the *Independent,* London: Independent.co.uk, 6 February [Source: http://argument.independent.co.uk/regular_columnists/hamish_mcrae/story.jsp?story=369238, Accessed: 06/02/03].

26   *SN* (2003), 'SN Global Top 25', New York: Supermarket News [Source: http://www.supermarketnews.com/sntop25.htm, Accessed: 03/10/03].

27   Rowell, A. (2000), 'SUCKERS – Why Britain Can't Afford Wal-Mart', the *Ecologist*, 22/09/2000 [Source: http://www.andyrowell.com/articles/suckers_walmart.html, Accessed: 11/09/03].

28   *Race to the Top* (2003), How Ethical are our Supermarkets? We can't tell you, London: International Institute for Environment and Developemnt [Source:http://www.racetothetop.org/documents/PR20031125.pdf] Accessed: 01/12/03].

29   *Race to the Top* (2003).

30   Young, W., Quist, J., Toth, K., Anderson, K. & Green, K. (2001), 'Exploring Sustainable Futures Through 'Design Orienting Scenarios' – The Case Shopping, Cooking And Eating', *Journal of Sustainable Product Design*, 1, (2), pp.117–29.

Index

Index

About the Author

William Young is the co-author (with Richard Welford) of *Ethical Shopping: Where to Shop, What to Buy and What to Do to Make a Difference* (Fusion Press, 2002). He is lecturer in Environment, Sustainable Development and Business at the School of the Environment, University of Leeds. He is the UK principle expert for the British Standards Institute, drafting an international environmental management standard, and is on the advisory board for Corporate Social Responsibility and Environmental Management journal.